P9-DDG-245

Honoring Diverse Teaching Styles

A Guide for Supervisors

Edward Pajak

ASCD

Association for Supervision and Curriculum Development ❖ Alexandria, Virginia USA

Association for Supervision and Curriculum Development
1703 N. Beauregard St. • Alexandria, VA 22311-1714 USA
Telephone: 800-933-2723 or 703-578-9600 • Fax: 703-575-5400
Web site: http://www.ascd.org • E-mail: member@ascd.org

Gene R. Carter, *Executive Director;* Nancy Modrak, *Director of Publishing;* Julie Houtz, *Director of Book Editing & Production;* Deborah Siegel, *Project Manager;* Georgia McDonald, *Senior Graphic Designer;* Keith Demmons, *Typesetter;* Tracey Smith, *Production Manager.*

Copyright © 2003 by Edward Pajak. All rights reserved. No part of this publication may be reproduced or transmitted in any form or by any means, electronic or mechanical, including photocopy, recording, or any information storage and retrieval system, without permission from ASCD. Readers who wish to duplicate material copyrighted by ASCD may do so for a small fee by contacting the Copyright Clearance Center (CCC), 222 Rosewood Dr., Danvers, MA 01923, USA (telephone: 978-750-8400; fax: 978-750-4470; Web: http://www.copyright.com). ASCD has authorized the CCC to collect such fees on its behalf. Requests to reprint rather than photocopy should be directed to ASCD's permissions office at 703-578-9600.

Cover art copyright © 2003 by ASCD.

ASCD publications present a variety of viewpoints. The views expressed or implied in this book should not be interpreted as official positions of the Association.

Printed in the United States of America.

May 2003 member book (p). ASCD Premium, Comprehensive, and Regular members periodically receive ASCD books as part of their membership benefits. No. FY03-07.

ISBN: 0-87120-776-1   ASCD product no.: 103012
ASCD member price: $18.95   nonmember price: $22.95

Library of Congress Cataloging-in-Publication Data
Pajak, Edward, 1947–
   Honoring diverse teaching styles : a guide for supervisors / Edward Pajak.
      p. cm.
Includes bibliographical references and index.
   ISBN 0-87120-776-1 (alk. paper)
   1. School supervision—United States. 2. Effective teaching–United States. 3. Teachers–In-service training–United States. I. Association for Supervision and Curriculum Development. II. Title.

   LB2806.4.P355 2003
   371.2'03—dc21

                                        2003004503

12 11 10 09 08 07 06 05 04 03   12 11 10 9 8 7 6 5 4 3 2 1

Honoring Diverse Teaching Styles

A Guide for Supervisors

Foreword *by Peyton Williams* v

Preface vii

Acknowledgments ix

1. Understanding the Clinical Cycle 1

2. The Clinical Cycle and
   Psychological Functions 10

3. Experiences of Teaching 22

4. Languages, Dialects,
   and the Clinical Cycle 36

5. Communicating Successfully
   with *All* Teachers 48

6. Speaking the Languages and Dialects 62

7. Developing an Integrated Style 79

Appendix A:
   Clinical Dialect Preference Survey 95

Appendix B:
   Communicating with Teachers Worksheets 100

References 108

Movie References 112

Index 113

About the Author 118

Foreword

by Peyton Williams

This important monograph appears at a time when educators face the challenge of ensuring high-quality instruction for every student, while simultaneously recruiting and socializing an unprecedented number of new and second-career teachers into the professional ranks. Edward Pajak has written a refreshingly original book that can help school practitioners and teacher educators address this dual challenge by shifting clinical supervision to an entirely new level.

Pajak successfully combines all of the major models of clinical supervision around the central concept of teaching styles. Vivid and powerful images that illustrate different styles of teaching are drawn from unforgettable films like *Stand and Deliver, Kindergarten Cop, Mr. Holland's Opus, Dangerous Minds*, and *Music of the Heart.* Useful tools and practical suggestions are provided, as well, for improving communication with teachers whose varied ways of thinking and speaking are compared to different languages and dialects.

At a more practical level, this very readable book demonstrates how alienation, apathy, disillusionment, and despair can be successfully countered through clinical cycles of engagement, empathy, encouragement, and empowerment. A potent schoolwide strategy for improving instruction is described that engages beginning and veteran teachers in differentiated learning teams, which accommodate their preferences for experiential learning, reflection, construction of meaning, and experimentation.

Honoring Diverse Teaching Styles: A Guide for Supervisors adheres to the premise that those who provide supervisory support "should strive to work with teachers in ways that are consistent with how teachers are expected to work with students—by celebrating diversity and responding to that diversity in ways that enhance learning for all." This sentiment and the practices it engenders continue ASCD's long-standing commitment to democratic principles and respect for creativity, cooperation, decentralization, and individual differences.

Peyton Williams
President, 2002–2003
Association for Supervision
and Curriculum Development

Preface

Psychologists have known for many years that human beings differ from one another in the ways that we process information. Some people easily get involved with their physical and social environments, while others prefer to stand back and get a more distanced, intuitive grasp of the big picture. Some people carefully think things through in a step-by-step manner before making a decision, while others are more apt to trust their feelings or be guided by personal values. Until now, these insights into human differences have been applied mainly to understanding student learning styles, as well as in human resource training and career counseling. This book proposes that clinical supervisors can improve their success by using "languages" and communication "dialects" that complement the experiences and styles of the teachers with whom they work and the goals they hope to achieve.

Choosing the correct communication strategy has been a central concern among theorists and practitioners of clinical supervision for decades. While most agree that the individual needs of teachers should be considered, experts conflict significantly in the specific advice that they offer. Some advise supervisors to refrain from being overly direct when working with an inexperienced teacher so that the novice has opportunity to develop an independent professional identity. Others assert that a direct supervisory communication style is exactly the tonic for inexperienced newcomers who may be struggling for survival. Rather than prescribing absolutes, an understanding of psychological functions can move clinical supervision beyond this *either, or* dichotomy between direct and indirect styles of communication and allows us to accept *both, and* a range of alternatives that may be appropriate under different sets of circumstances.

The fundamental belief guiding this book is simple, yet powerful. Clinical supervisors, no less than teachers, should make a deliberate effort to honor and legitimate perspectives and strategies that differ from their own preferred tendencies for perceiving and judging reality. That is to say, supervisors should strive to work with teachers in ways that are consistent with how teachers are expected to work with students—by celebrating diversity and responding to that diversity in ways that enhance learning for all. By doing so, clinical supervisors can make better decisions about the most appropriate approaches to use when working with teachers who demonstrate different styles of thinking and teaching. Clinical supervisors can thereby improve their own success in helping teachers to teach more effectively.

Acknowledgments

My sincere gratitude is extended to the many people who offered ideas, suggestions, and constructive criticism during the preparation of this book, including Yolanda Abel, Kathy Bovard, Donna Butler, Deborah Carran, David Champagne, Matt Dammann, Frank Duffy, Jeanne Paynter, Gilda Martinez, Tonya Osmond, Mary Somers, Amy Wilson, and the students enrolled in my Teacher Leadership Seminar. I also want to thank the ASCD editorial staff for their confidence in this project, and especially Deborah Siegel for her close attention and helpfulness during the editing process.

As always, my love goes out to my wife, Diane, and to our children, Alexandra and Zachary, along with warm appreciation for their encouragement after reading an early draft. Zack, in particular, deserves special thanks for sharing with me his insights and extensive knowledge of movies.

Finally, I dedicate this work to my mother, Florence, and to the memory of my father, Edward, both of whom always allowed me to be who I am.

Thanksgiving Day, 2002
Clarksville, Maryland

1

Understanding the Clinical Cycle

Sally Taylor has taught 5th grade for 19 years in the same school and has always done things her own way. That is not to say she hasn't changed or improved over time, only that she is used to making independent decisions about what happens in her own classroom. Sally's instruction has been described by several principals over the years as "highly structured" and "teacher centered." Everything about her lessons is carefully planned and well executed, but she leaves little room for spontaneity or student initiative.

In recent years, some parents have occasionally complained that Sally puts too many demands on her students' time with daily homework assignments and frequent quizzes. But the majority of parents seem satisfied that their children are getting a traditional education, similar to what they experienced when they were 5th graders. Indeed, Sally has also been described by more than one principal as a "very effective" teacher. In fact, early in her career and right after getting tenure, Sally was recognized at her school as Teacher of the Year.

For the entire year that she has been principal, Flora Seager has encouraged teachers to allow students to work in self-directed groups as often as possible. After reading several books on cooperative learning while working on her master's degree, and believing strongly in the importance of young people developing strong interpersonal skills and positive attitudes toward others, Flora reflected on her own eight years of teaching at several different grade levels. She became firmly convinced that elementary students learn best in social contexts, and she resolved to promote instructional practices that enable students to do so.

Several days ago, Flora visited Sally's classroom for an annual end-of-year observation. She had intended to observe the classrooms of all the teachers several times during the school year, but found that her duties as a first-year principal kept getting in her way. Upon entering Sally's classroom, Flora was a little dismayed to see that the students' desks were all lined up in straight rows. But she was absolutely horrified when she happened to notice later that the students' seats were arranged alphabetically.

Sally began the lesson by explaining its purpose to her students. She then reviewed what they had learned the day before and led a very orderly discussion about the climates, natural resources, and economies of several South American countries. She paused occasionally to write key ideas on the board at the front of the room; the students dutifully copied this information into their notebooks.

The next day, the postobservation conference began politely enough. But after Flora mentioned that the straight rows and alphabetical seating chart prevented students from interacting with each other, the meeting became an increasingly heated debate about the merits and shortcomings of direct instruction versus cooperative learning. Feeling more frustrated by the minute, Flora made a general comment at one point about "out-of-date teaching practices and the need for everyone to change with the times." Taking this remark as personal criticism, Sally responded by saying that she believed nothing of any value could ever come from 5th grade students "getting together and pooling their ignorance."

Shocked by a statement that she thought might border on insubordination, and wanting to regain some control, Flora responded by saying, "Well, as the principal of this school, I have certain expectations about instruction that I would like to see followed."

Never one to back down, Sally stared directly at the principal and calmly said, "I've been teaching in this school for almost 20 years. This is only your first year here. During my career, I've seen a lot of classroom fads come and go. The education pendulum just keeps swinging back and forth. And every time we get a new principal, the teachers are all expected to start chasing another bandwagon? Whatever happens to be 'in' this year is 'out' the next year."

Sally then stood up and collected her belongings, signaling her intention to leave. "If you happen to be principal of this school five years from now," she paused to say, "you'll see that my teaching won't be out of date. By that time, I'll be right back on the cutting edge!"

Flora felt frustrated and defeated. She wondered exactly what had gone wrong and what she could have done differently.

What Is the Problem?

Despite our best efforts, educators' conversations about best practice often deteriorate into opposing positions, both of which may have merit— individual versus whole-group instruction, phonics versus whole language, cognitive versus affective outcomes, mastery of facts versus higher-order thinking, acquisition of basic skills versus creative expression, pre-determined content versus construction of knowledge. The immediate result of all these conflicting perspectives is that we often talk right past each another, or try to persuade each other that our viewpoint is correct, instead of taking time to truly understand the other point of view (Glickman, 2001; Mosston & Ashworth, 1990; Sergiovanni, 1995). The more serious and long-term consequence is that all this constant debate and turmoil makes it impossible for educators to experience the uninterrupted internal narratives needed to develop integrated professional identities and a coherent professional culture, both of which are necessary to inspire us and lead us to greatness.

Similarly, when educators talk about or try to use clinical supervision, disagreements often arise that become barriers to understanding and success. Although people may agree in principle that teachers can benefit from expert assistance and feedback about their classroom performance, communication begins to break down as soon as details enter the conversation about *what* good teaching looks like. Even the experts cannot agree about *who* should provide feedback to teachers, *how* it should be delivered, *when* in a teacher's career supervision is most helpful, or even *why* clinical supervision is important. At times it almost seems that people are speaking different languages or dialects. And, in a sense, they are. This book proposes that the theory of psychological functions introduced by Carl Jung (1971) and popularized by others (e.g., Briggs & Myers, 1977; Keirsey, 1998) can bring conceptual clarity to the field of clinical supervision and, more importantly, serve as a guide to principals, mentors, and peer coaches as they seek to improve their communication skills.

The fundamental belief guiding this book is simple, yet powerful: clinical supervisors of instruction, no less than teachers, should make a deliberate effort to honor and legitimate perspectives and practices that differ from their own preferred styles of perceiving, judging, and communicating about reality. This book explains how consideration of teachers' teaching styles during the clinical supervision cycle gives teachers greater choice and voice and can contribute to schoolwide professional development through the creation of learning environments that address particular teaching styles. Style-guided supervisory practice also makes professional development more coherent because it is consistent with instructional and assessment practices that are associated with differentiated learning.

The Truth About Supervision in Education

Some educators are reluctant to use the word "supervision," because they incorrectly associate it with a hierarchical relationship rooted in an industrial model of schooling. On the contrary, Edward C. Elliott, an early 20th-century educator, described supervision in schools as being closely related to "the democratic motive of American education" (Elliott, 1914, p. 2). He clearly distinguished "centralization of administrative power," which he said stifled creativity and individuality in school, from "*decentralized, cooperative, expert*, supervision" (p. 78). By the 1920s, no fewer than five textbooks emphasized democracy as a guiding principle of supervision in education (Ayer & Barr, 1928; Barr & Burton, 1926; Burton, 1927; Hosic, 1920; Stone, 1929).

In his classic study *Education and the Cult of Efficiency*, Raymond Callahan (1962) showed how educational administration was influenced by industrial logic just prior to World War I. Rarely recognized by contemporary authors, however, is the fact that the resulting scientific management movement had comparatively little influence on supervision in education because "the problems of supervision and teaching method were not readily amenable to . . . the management frame of reference." Callahan also explained that supervision distinguished itself from both administration and industrial logic in the 1930s by aligning itself with the process of curriculum development and "a new organization, the Association for Supervision and Curriculum Development" (Callahan & Button, 1964). It is in this traditional democratic spirit of supervision in education and its long-standing respect for creativity, cooperation, decentralization, and individual difference that this book is written.

What Is Clinical Supervision?

The use of clinical supervision as a method for improving instruction has a fairly recent history in the United States. The earliest application began with Morris Cogan and Robert Goldhammer at Harvard University in the 1960s and continued later at the University of Pittsburgh and other institutions. Their efforts were stimulated by frustrations they encountered as university supervisors trying to help beginning teachers succeed. Goldhammer and Cogan borrowed the term "clinical supervision" from the medical profession, where it has been used for decades to describe a process for perfecting the specialized knowledge and skills of practitioners. Essentially, clinical supervision in education involves a teacher receiving information from a colleague who has observed the teacher's performance and who serves as both a mirror and a sounding board to enable the teacher to critically examine and possibly alter his or her own professional practice. Although classroom observations are often conducted by university supervisors or principals, clinical supervision is increasingly used successfully by mentor teachers, peer coaches, and teacher colleagues who believe that a fresh perspective will help to improve classroom success.

Despite many variations that have been proposed over the years, the basic five-stage clinical supervision sequence suggested by Goldhammer (1969) remains most widely known. The tasks of the teacher and the supervisor during each stage and key questions that both ought to consider are summarized below.

Stage 1—Pre-observation Conference

Teacher's Task: To mentally rehearse and orally describe the upcoming lesson, including the purpose and the content, what the teacher will do, and what students are expected to do and learn.

Clinical Supervisor's Task: To learn about and understand what the teacher has in mind for the lesson to be taught by asking probing and clarifying questions.

Questions to Consider: What type of data will be recorded (e.g., teacher questions, student behaviors, movement patterns)? How will data be recorded (e.g., video or audio recording, verbatim transcript, anecdotal notes, checklist)? Who will do what in the subsequent stages?

Stage 2—Classroom Observation

Teacher's Task: To teach the lesson as well as possible.

Clinical Supervisor's Task: To record events occurring during the lesson as accurately as possible.

Stage 3—Data Analysis and Strategy

Teacher's Task: To help make sense of the data (if directly involved in this stage).

Clinical Supervisor's Task: To make some sense of the raw data and to develop a plan for the conference.

Questions to Consider: What patterns are evident in the data? Are any critical incidents or turning points obvious? What strengths did the teacher exhibit? Were any techniques especially successful? Are there any concerns about the lesson? Which patterns, events, and concerns are most important to address? Which patterns, events, and concerns can be addressed in the time available? How will the conference begin? How will the conference end?

Stage 4—Conference

Teacher's Task: To critically examine his or her own teaching with an open mind and to tentatively plan for the next lesson.

Clinical Supervisor's Task: To help clarify and build upon the teacher's understanding of the behaviors and events that occurred in the classroom.

Questions to Consider: What patterns and critical incidents are evident in the data? What is the relationship between these events and student learning? Were any unanticipated or unintended outcomes evident? What will the teacher do differently for the next class meeting (e.g., new objectives, methods, content, materials, teacher behaviors, student activities, or assessments)?

Stage 5—Postconference Analysis

Teacher's Task: To provide honest feedback to the clinical supervisor about how well the clinical supervision cycle went.

Clinical Supervisor's Task: To critically examine his or her own performance during the clinical supervision cycle.

Questions to Consider: Generally, how well did the clinical supervision cycle go? What worked well? What did not work well? If you could do it again, what would you do differently? What will you do differently during the next clinical supervision cycle?

The Four Families of Clinical Supervision

After Goldhammer proposed the five-stage sequence, which he distilled from a more extensive series of eight phases advocated by Cogan, other scholars began commenting and elaborating on the clinical supervision cycle from a variety of perspectives. Many authors have written about clinical supervision during the last several decades. The most popular approaches, however, can be classified into four "families" that share certain qualities (See Figure 1.1).

Figure 1.1

Four Families of Clinical Supervision

Original Clinical Models

The original models proposed by Goldhammer and Cogan offer a blend of empirical, behavioral, phenomenological, and developmental perspectives. These approaches emphasize the importance of collegial relationships with teachers, cooperative discovery of meaning, and development of unique teaching styles.

Artistic/Humanistic Models

The perspectives of Eisner and Blumberg are based on aesthetic and existential principles. These approaches forsake step-by-step procedures and emphasize open interpersonal relations and personal intuition, artistry, and idiosyncrasy. Supervisors are encouraged to help teachers understand the artistic and expressive richness of teaching.

Technical/Didactic Models

The approaches to clinical supervision proposed by Acheson and Gall and by Hunter draw heavily on findings from process-product and effective teaching research. These approaches emphasize techniques of observation and feedback that reinforce certain "effective" behaviors or predetermined models of teaching to which teachers attempt to conform.

Developmental/Reflective Models

The models of Glickman, Costa and Garmston, Zeichner and Liston, Garman, Smyth, and Waite are sensitive to individual differences and the social, organizational, political, and cultural contexts of teaching. These authors call on supervisors to encourage reflection among teachers, foster growth, and promote justice and equity.

Adapted from Pajak (2000)

The four "families" of clinical supervision depicted in Figure 1.1 emerged chronologically, pretty much in the order that they are listed. The "original clinical models" outlined by Goldhammer (1969) and Cogan (1973) in the late 1960s and early 1970s, for example, were followed during the mid- to late-1970s by the "artistic/humanistic" models of Eisner

(1979) and Blumberg (1974). In turn, the "technical/didactic" models advocated by Acheson and Gall (1980) and Hunter (1984) gained ascendancy in the early to mid-1980s, and were themselves followed by the "developmental/reflective" models. The models in this last category arose during the mid-1980s and continued proliferating through the 1990s, including those proposed by Glickman (1985), Zeichner and Liston (1987), Costa and Garmston (1994), and others (Garman, 1986; Smyth, 1985; Waite, 1995).

These four families of clinical supervision differ from one another in the purposes toward which they strive, their relative emphasis on objectivity versus subjectivity, the type of data collected and the procedures for recording it, the number and series of steps or stages involved, the degree of control exercised by the supervisor versus the teacher, and the nature and structure of pre- and postobservation conferences.

More detailed descriptions and comparisons among the different models in these families have been published elsewhere (Pajak, 2000). The appropriateness of these models and families of clinical supervision for working with teachers who differ in the ways that they perceive and relate to the world are explored in the chapters that follow.

Discussion Questions

1. What is the underlying cause of disagreement between Sandy Taylor and Flora Seager, the teacher and principal introduced at the beginning of this chapter?

2. How might Flora have approached her conference with Sandy differently to keep communication from breaking down?

3. What has been your experience with classroom observation and feedback during your career?

4. What questions might Flora use to elicit Sally's belief system about teaching and her willingness to examine its effectiveness?

The Clinical Cycle and Psychological Functions

Among many other important discoveries related to conscious and unconscious mental processes, the Swiss psychologist Carl Jung proposed that people exhibit four psychological "functions" with respect to their perceptions. Two of these functions, intuition (N) and sensing (S), describe the ways we gather data about and perceive reality, while another two functions, thinking (T) and feeling (F), refer to the ways that we appraise or judge the reality that we perceive.

Although gathering data and making judgments about perceptions are obviously central issues for those who practice clinical supervision, surprisingly little has been written about applications of Jung's work to this field. Champagne and Hogan (1995) have done more to apply Jung's formulations to clinical supervision than anyone else. Their book includes a useful instrument for assessing psychological type and function, and they speculate about the effect these mental processes have on both teaching and supervision. The concept of psychological functions already productively informs other areas of study, including learning styles (Silver, Strong, & Perini, 2000), leadership (Fitzgerald & Kirby, 1997), and organizational dynamics (Hirsch & Kummerow, 1998), all of which have clear relevance for understanding classrooms and schools. Recently, a number of scholars have suggested that concepts derived from the psychology of Carl Jung may offer a promising perspective for understanding and improving the practice of instructional supervision (Champagne &

Hogan, 1995; Garmston, Lipton, & Kaiser, 1998; Hawthorne & Hoffman, 1998; Norris, 1991; Oja & Reiman, 1998; Sergiovanni & Starratt, 1998; Shapiro & Blumberg, 1998). It seems obvious, therefore, that the implications of Jung's formulations for clinical supervision are worth exploring further.

Most educators are already familiar with the concept of learning styles from the work of people like Anthony Gregorc (1982), David Kolb (1984), Bernice McCarthy (1982; 1990), and others. Many teachers and administrators have taken the Myers-Briggs Type Indicator (1996), the Keirsey Temperament Sorter (Keirsey, 1998), or another instrument designed to identify an individual's personality type or style of thinking and learning. The theory behind all these conceptions of style and type can be traced directly to the work of Carl Jung.

In his book *Man and His Symbols*, Jung (1979) describes the four psychological functions—sensing, thinking, feeling, and intuiting—in the following way:

> *Sensation* (i.e., sense perception) tells you that something exists; *thinking* tells you what it is; *feeling* tells you whether it is agreeable or not; and *intuition* tells you whence it comes and where it is going (p. 49).

Elsewhere, Jung (1971) compared the four functions to the points on a compass and suggested that the interplay among the four functions was as indispensable for psychological orientation and discovery as a compass is for navigation. The functions are displayed in a compasslike configuration in Figure 2.1 to illustrate their relationship to each other.

Sensing and Intuiting

People use both sensing and intuiting to record perceptions about their environments? The sensing function is concrete and draws directly on our five senses—sight, smell, taste, hearing, and touch—to tell us about the world around us. The sensing function focuses on facts and details about

Figure 2.1

The Four Functions as Compass Points

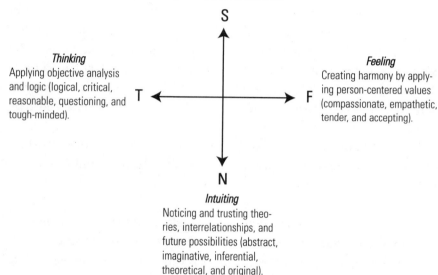

Sensing
Noticing and trusting facts, details, and present realities (concrete, realistic, practical, experiential, and traditional).

S

Thinking
Applying objective analysis and logic (logical, critical, reasonable, questioning, and tough-minded).

T

Feeling
Creating harmony by applying person-centered values (compassionate, empathetic, tender, and accepting).

F

N

Intuiting
Noticing and trusting theories, interrelationships, and future possibilities (abstract, imaginative, inferential, theoretical, and original).

our present reality. The intuiting function, in contrast, is more abstract and relies on the intellect to make wholistic inferences about the possibilities inherent in a situation. The intuiting function, sometimes called our "sixth" sense, considers larger concepts and possibilities.

We all rely on both sensing and intuiting to make sense of reality. We depend on the sensing function when we want to see the trees, for example, and on the intuiting function when we want to see the forest. But we differ from each other in the degree to which we rely on one function or the other. Some people want to know exactly how much money they have in their checking accounts, while others are satisfied with only a general notion of what is available for them to spend. This preference for one function over the other is sometimes compared to our preference for using our right hand or our left (Kroeger and Thuesen, 1988).

According to Jung (1971), people who draw primarily on intuition to collect data and perceive reality are interested in ideas and theories, untried possibilities, and what is new. They quickly become bored with specifics, details, data, and facts that are unrelated to concepts. Intuitive people tend to think and communicate with spontaneous leaps of imagination and may omit or neglect details. In contrast, those who draw on the sensing function to gather data and perceive reality prefer focusing on what is real, concrete, and tangible in the here and now. They tend to be more concerned with facts and data than with theory and abstractions. Sensing people think and communicate carefully and accurately, referring to and emphasizing facts and details, but they often miss seeing the gestalt or big picture (Kroeger & Thuesen, 1988).

Thinking and Feeling

Thinking and feeling are both described by Jung (1971) as rational functions. By this he meant that we use them to make judgments about our perceptions of the world. Most people have little trouble recognizing that thinking is a rational function, but are somewhat puzzled by Jung's use of the word feeling in this way (Stevens, 1994). It is important to understand that Jung was not referring to emotions when he described the feeling function:

> When I use the word "feeling" in contrast to "thinking," I refer to a judgment of value—for instance, agreeable or disagreeable, good or bad, and so on. Feeling according to this definition is not an emotion (which, as the word conveys, is involuntary). *Feeling* as I mean it is (like thinking) a *rational* (i.e., ordering) function (Jung, 1979, p. 49).

One way to understand the difference between the thinking and feeling functions is in terms of the distinction we make between truth and beauty. The first virtue appeals to our brain, while the second appeals to our heart, and we use both at times when making decisions or judgments. The thinking function is concerned with logic, structure, and cause-and-effect relationships. With thinking, conclusions are reached through logical analysis. The feeling function, in contrast, relates to what is subjectively experienced as pleasant or unpleasant, desirable or undesirable, exciting or boring. With feeling, conclusions are based on personal values and preferences.

Technology has given us a concept and term that was not available in Jung's time—*information processing*. It may be meaningful today, therefore, to consider thinking and feeling as two distinct ways that we process information about the world that we perceive through the sensing and intuiting functions.

Again, all of us rely on both thinking and feeling to make sense of reality. But we differ in the degree to which we depend on one function or the other. Some people make a decision about buying a new car primarily on the basis of considerations like cost and consumer ratings (thinking), while others are more strongly influenced by preferences for styling and color, or consideration of the vehicle's impact on the environment (feeling).

People who favor thinking over feeling when making judgments about the reality they perceive prefer using evidence, analysis, and logic. They are more concerned with being rational than with empathy, emotions, and values. Thinking types communicate in an orderly and linear manner, emphasizing if-then and cause-effect linkages. On the other hand, those who prefer using feeling to guide their judgments do so on the basis of empathy, warmth, personal convictions, and a consistent value system that underlies all their decision processes. They are more interested in people, emotions, aesthetics, and harmony than with logic, analysis, or attaining impersonal goals. Feeling people communicate by expressing personal likes and dislikes as well as feelings about what is good versus bad, or right versus wrong.

Psychological Functions and Classroom Observation

Imagine that a science teacher is teaching an introductory lesson to a 9th grade class about how animals evolve physical adaptations in response to the environment. After he reviews the various climatic areas and habitats on earth, the teacher asks his students to share their observations of animal life from experiences they have had when traveling in different parts of their state and in other states. The teacher also distributes a number of artifacts, which the students handle and pass around the room as the lesson unfolds. Now, imagine that four different people—a sensing type, a thinking type, a feeling type, and an intuiting type—all observed the lesson and reported on what they saw.

A sensing observer will provide the most factual account of what happened, describing and emphasizing objective reality:

> A row of aquariums and terrariums holding living creatures lined one classroom wall. The opposite wall was decorated with astronomy charts and bright posters explaining the contributions of famous scientists. The teacher began the lesson by writing the objective on the board at the front of the classroom with a blue marker. He pointed to a color-coded world map while briefly describing different climatic regions and ecological systems. The teacher asked the students if any of them had ever visited a beach at the ocean. Nine students raised their hands and he called on three of them to describe the evidence of animal life they saw there. The teacher next asked if any students had visited the mountains. This time, seven students raised their hands. He again called on three students, different ones this time, to describe their experiences and the animals they had seen. As the discussion continued, the teacher allowed the students to touch and examine the wide jaws of a shark, an eagle's sharp talons and beak, and the hard, smooth shell of a tortoise.

A thinking observer will offer an interpretive account of events as they happened:

> The teacher focused students' attention on what they were to learn by writing the objective on the board. Activities that followed were designed to contribute to the accomplishment of the lesson's objective. The teacher heightened the students' curiosity and interest by allowing them to handle and pass around preserved remains from several animals and encouraged student participation by asking them about different places they had visited. He made an effort to involve a sizeable number of students while carefully ensuring that the lesson stayed focused. The students appeared motivated by the chance to describe their personal experiences with animal life while on vacation in different geographic and climatic regions. The teacher then related the students' observations to the objective.

A feeling observer will respond by making personal value judgments about the lesson:

> This was an excellent lesson! The teacher used a variety of exciting methods that actively engaged the students in learning. The students were clearly excited when given an opportunity to share personal memories of family vacations with their classmates. A few seemed a little squeamish and were initially reluctant to touch the remains of dead animals that the teacher handed out. But all the students enthusiastically shared comments with each other as they passed the fragile objects back and forth. The openness and participation encouraged a stimulating and lively conversation. I enjoyed the lesson tremendously myself!

An intuiting observer will explain events in the classroom concep-tually and will project implications for the future:

> The teacher employed an inductive/discovery method of instruction. The lesson was highly structured and teacher-centered, but the teacher drew on the students' personal experiences to provide a relevant foundation for their understanding. Student involvement and creativity might have been increased by allowing the students to handle the artifacts beforehand and then having them pose hypotheses about the utility of the adaptations for ensuring the survival of these animals. A good follow-up lesson would be to have the students consider how humans change the environment and then speculate about how those changes influence environmental habitats and animals.

How the Four Functions Interact

Although every person is born with a capacity to exercise all four psychological functions, most of us gradually come to rely more frequently on a single function from each pair. The function that we rely on most often is called our dominant or superior function. The dominant function—sensing or intuiting, thinking or feeling—is supported by an auxiliary function from the other pair. That is to say, if our dominant function (the one that we depend on most often) is intuition, then our supporting function will be either thinking or feeling. If our dominant function is feeling, then our auxiliary function will be either sensing or intuiting. The functions that are not often used remain undeveloped and become associated with what Jung called our *shadow,* a place in our unconscious where we try to bury qualities that we reject as inconsistent with our conscious image of ourselves.

The relationship among the four functions can be understood by way of an analogy. Imagine that the four functions are four people out for a drive in an automobile (see Figure 2.2). If intuiting (N) is the dominant function, you would find it in the driver's seat right behind the steering wheel. Intuition is clearly in control of where the car is headed, how fast it is going, and when and where it may stop. If thinking (T) is the auxiliary function, you would find it in the front passenger's seat. Thinking may be along for the ride, but it can contribute as a navigator, pointing out interesting landmarks and hazards along the highway, and it might even get to drive occasionally. Meanwhile, sensing (S) and feeling (F) are huddled like small children in the back seat. Their contribution to the drive is minimal, because they are undeveloped. As passengers, they have difficulty seeing the road and are far from the controls. They may spend most of the time just passively watching the landscape go by. We can become more complete and effective as human beings, according to Jung, if we can learn to use these undeveloped functions in our daily lives instead of neglecting them.

Figure 2.2

How the Functions Interact

The Function Pairs and the Families of Clinical Supervision

When the psychological processes of getting information and making decisions combine and interact (see Figure 2.3), four possible function pairs result: sensory-thinking (S-T), sensory-feeling (S-F), intuitive-thinking (N-T), and intuitive-feeling (N-F). These four combinations determine how individuals relate to the world that they encounter. The combinations also correspond quite closely with the four families of clinical supervision described earlier.

Figure 2.3

Function Pairs and Clinical Supervision Families

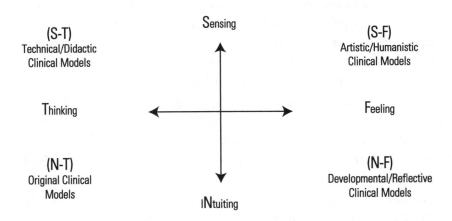

Sensing

(S-T)
Technical/Didactic
Clinical Models

(S-F)
Artistic/Humanistic
Clinical Models

Thinking

Feeling

(N-T)
Original Clinical
Models

(N-F)
Developmental/Reflective
Clinical Models

INtuiting

People who display an intuitive-thinking (N-T) function pair, for example, are concerned with competence and tend to concentrate on ideas, possibilities, and the future. They are guided by theoretical concepts and work by testing hypotheses. N-Ts are likely to consider the larger context and are distressed by what they view as incorrect or faulty principles. This worldview most closely parallels the original clinical models developed by Goldhammer (1969) and Cogan (1973).

In comparison, individuals who display a sensory-feeling (S-F) combination are concerned with harmony and want very much to be helpful to others. They focus attention on the present and facts, but are most concerned with people. S-Fs like to provide support and are guided by a sense of service. They work by meeting people's needs and are troubled by conflict and disagreements. An S-F orientation most closely resembles the artistic/humanistic family of models represented by Eisner (1979) and Blumberg (1974).

People possessing a sensory-thinking (S-T) orientation mainly strive to be efficient. They focus on the present and facts, and attend closely to current reality. They prefer to follow established policies and procedures and believe that their work and the work of others is facilitated by having such processes and structures in place. S-Ts want to see results produced and are annoyed when work is done incorrectly. The technical/didactic models of Acheson and Gall (1980) and Hunter (1984) match up well with this perspective. Other examples include Harris and Hill's (1982) DeTek diagnostic process and Danielson's (1996) framework for teaching.

Finally, people who possess an intuitive-feeling (N-F) combination seek to empower others and are strongly concerned with the future, people, and possibilities. Guided by ideals that they believe are worthy, N-Fs work by expressing and acting on their values. These individuals seek to promote growth and are troubled when values are ignored or when values that they consider improper predominate. The developmental/reflective models, represented by a range of authors (e.g., Costa & Garmston, 1994; Garman, 1986; Glickman, 1985; Smyth, 1985; Waite, 1995; Zeichner & Liston, 1987) are associated with the N-F combination of functions.

Understanding how these approaches differ is important because clinical supervisors of instruction, no less than teachers, should make a deliberate effort to honor and legitimate perspectives and strategies that are not consistent with their own preferred tendencies for perceiving, judging, and communicating about reality. That is to say, practitioners of clinical supervision should strive to work with teachers in ways that are consistent with how teachers are expected to work with students—by celebrating diversity and responding to that diversity in ways that enhance learning for all.

The concept of psychological functions helps illustrate how the four clinical supervision families (introduced in Chapter 1) actually complement each other, despite the obvious differences among them. This understanding can provide educators with a useful foundation from which to build more informed, precise, caring, and meaningful supervisory practice in education.

Discussion Questions

1. What does the concept of psychological functions tell us about how people learn?

2. Should clinical supervisors of instruction take psychological functions into consideration when they work with teachers? Why or why not?

3. What advice would you now give to Flora Seager (the principal who was introduced in Chapter 1) when she works with a teacher like Sally Taylor?

4. How can the concept of psychological functions help Flora and Sally work more successfully together?

3

Experiences of Teaching

The role of teacher is defined in part by cultural expectations, social norms, and organizational rules that originate and operate from outside the classroom. However, the specific enactment of the teacher role depends on deliberate choices made by individuals in that role and on powerful unconscious patterns of behavior. These unconscious patterns express the internal psychological makeup of individuals, and determine the manner in which they relate to the world and to others around them. The external expectations, norms, and rules, however, also reinforce the enactment of certain patterns and suppress the enactment of others.

The perspective of teaching represented in this book is different from most others, which begin with and concentrate on external realities, and prescribe "one best way" for teachers to think and to behave. The interpretations presented here begin with and focus on the subjective experience and internal realities of being a teacher, and accept a diverse range of thoughts, behaviors, and feelings about teaching as normal, appropriate, and desirable.

Variations on the Teaching Experience

Over many years, in both classroom and workshop settings, I have asked teachers to think and talk with each other about three questions:

"What does teaching mean to you?"

"What about teaching gives you the most satisfaction?"

"How do you know when you have been successful?"

Teachers' answers to these straightforward questions are often eloquent, complex, and inspiring, and suggest that teaching is much more than simply a job. For a great many people, teaching is nothing less than a way of living their lives. Teaching is closely connected, in other words, to how teachers view themselves as people. Indeed, what teachers do in their classrooms is tightly wrapped up with, and difficult to separate from, their very identities.

The responses that teachers offer to the questions that I pose also suggest that different people experience teaching in different ways. Some teachers place greater emphasis on imparting knowledge to students, for example, while others stress the importance of helping students discover knowledge for themselves. Some teachers believe in getting actively involved in students' personal lives, while others prefer to maintain a more distanced professional relationship. Some teachers dedicate themselves to social change and justice for all students, while others concentrate their efforts on individual students who show promise of becoming leaders of the next generation.

These different experiences of teaching can be understood, at least in part, through the lens of Jung's psychological functions. Figure 3.1 depicts four experiences or styles—*inventing, knowing, caring,* and *inspiring*—that highlight variations in how individuals perceive and process information, as well as how these differences give expression to the multiple purposes that can guide teaching.

Inventing teachers exhibit an intuiting-thinking preference. When asked to talk about teaching, they tend to emphasize the importance of "having students solve problems" and seeing "students apply their learning to real situations." *Knowing* teachers, who possess a sensing-thinking preference, are more likely to focus on "helping kids learn content" and believe they are successful when they see "students mastering the subject matter." *Caring* teachers, those who display a sensing-feeling preference, often say that "providing opportunities for student growth" is most important and

Figure 3.1

Teacher Goals and Psychological Functions

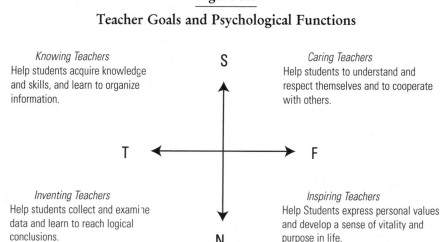

Knowing Teachers
Help students acquire knowledge
and skills, and learn to organize
information.

S

Caring Teachers
Help students to understand and
respect themselves and to cooperate
with others.

T ⟷ F

Inventing Teachers
Help students collect and examine
data and learn to reach logical
conclusions.

N

Inspiring Teachers
Help Students express personal values
and develop a sense of vitality and
purpose in life.

define success in terms of "building a classroom community." Finally, *inspiring* teachers possess an intuiting-feeling preference. They tend to view teaching as "an opportunity to shape the future" and describe success in terms of "seeing students make independent decisions."

Evidence of the Experiences

The four ways of experiencing teaching are clearly evident in the education literature. The *inventing* perspective is expressed, for example, in the scholarship of Jean Piaget, Jerome Bruner, and Hilda Taba; advocacy for the *knowing* viewpoint may be found in the writings of Benjamin Bloom, Mortimer Adler, and William Bennett; the importance of the *caring* attitude is explained to us by Carl Rogers, Nel Noddings, and Parker Palmer; while the *inspiring* stance is articulated in the work of Paulo Freire, Maxine Greene, and Henry Giroux, among others.

The curriculum and instruction literature, in particular, offers evidence of the four ways of experiencing teaching. Ornstein and Hunkins (1998), for example, identify four philosophies that provide the basis for curriculum in schools: perennialism, essentialism, progressivism, and reconstructionism. According to the philosophy of perennialism, they tell us the teacher's role is to cultivate the intellect by helping students to think rationally. Essentialism dictates that the teacher is an authority in his or her subject who promotes intellectual growth by communicating essential knowledge and skills. Progressivism favors a teacher who serves as a guide to students as they grapple with issues in a student-centered and cooperative social context. The philosophy of reconstructionism, finally, urges teachers to be agents of change who work with students to improve and reconstruct society (Ornstein & Hunkins, 1998, p. 56). The *inventing, knowing, caring,* and *inspiring* experiences of teaching, respectively, are clearly represented in these four schools of thought.

More than 25 ago, Eisner and Vallance (1974) similarly suggested that four conceptions of curriculum exist, each with a different purpose or emphasis: cognitive process, academic rationalism, self-actualization, and social reconstructionism. They linked these curriculum foci to four orientations or models of instruction—information processing, behavioral systems, personal, and social—that Joyce and Weil (1972) identified a few years earlier and which also parallel the four styles of teaching proposed here.

Joyce and Weil's four groups of teaching models vary in the degree to which they emphasize instructional and nurturant outcomes. Some are more efficient for conveying information or changing behavior, in other words, while others heighten awareness of feelings or improve interpersonal skills. As the name implies, the *information processing* category includes instructional models that aim to improve students' retention of information and teach them skills for higher-level thinking. The models in the *behavioral* group are derived from classical and operant conditioning, and rely on the stimulus-response-reinforcement sequence to encourage or extinguish patterns of student behavior. The *personal* models of teaching encompass strategies that are intended to develop students' self-concepts and improve intergroup attitudes and interactions. Finally, the *social* models include teaching strategies that emphasize cooperative learning and lead students in analyzing their own values as well as public policies (Joyce & Weil, 1986).

The four styles of teaching proposed in this book are also related to the learning styles identified by Kolb (1984) and Silver, Strong, and Perini (2000). These patterns of perceiving and processing information differ, however, in that they are shaped by and influence the experience of teaching instead of learning. Further distinctions among these groups can be identified as they relate to Jung's (1971) psychological functions (see Figure 3.2). Thus, the motives, purposes, frustrations, and rewards that teachers associate with teaching, and the very meaning that teaching has for their lives, vary considerably from one person to another (Reinsmith, 1992). However, the differentiation of experience is not infinite. Specific identifiable patterns of the experience of teaching can be discerned in the images found in popular fiction.

Figure 3.2
Comparison of the Four Teacher Types

	Inventing Teachers	Knowing Teachers	Caring Teachers	Inspiring Teachers
Focus on:	The future, possibilities, ideas	The present, facts, current reality	The present, people, facts	The future, people, ideals, possibilities
Strive to be:	Competent	Efficient	Helpful	Empowering
Guided by:	Theoretical concepts	Standards and procedures	Harmony and service to others	Ideals worth striving toward
Bothered by:	Incorrect or faulty principles	Work done incorrectly	Lack of harmony and balance	Absent or incorrect values
Work by:	Posing and testing hypotheses	Having processes and structures in place	Meeting people's needs	Expressing and acting on values
Like to:	Consider the big picture	Get results	Provide support	Promote growth

Images of the Experiences of Teaching

In his book, *The Hero with a Thousand Faces,* Joseph Campbell (1949) explains that the story of the hero has inspired people throughout history and across all cultures. The hero is a figure who arises when situations seem most bleak and hopeless, at times when the kingdom is in great peril. In order to restore hope, the hero begins a quest during which he or she encounters many trials, struggles against dragons and ogres, occasionally gets lost, obtains help from friendly strangers, descends to the underworld, and eventually emerges profoundly transformed. Innocence is lost, but courage is found, an enlightened understanding is won, and the kingdom is saved and restored in the end. The story of the hero holds lessons for everyone on how to live; indeed, it describes the process through which we form our adult identities. Therefore, every person's quest is different and each of us must find our own path.

Although the hero's journey is a timeless and universal myth, many of our specific views about heroes and heroic qualities come from representations that appear in popular culture. Jung (1969) tells us that such images are projections into the external world of patterns that originate in our collective unconscious minds.

Having been a teacher of one kind or another for all of my life, I have long followed with interest the ways that teachers are characterized by the media. Works of fiction depicting teachers have existed, of course, for many years. Throughout the 20th century, movies and video added striking visual impressions of teachers to the public imagination. Especially during the last 25 years, teachers have been portrayed as the central characters in many major motion pictures.

Most often, teachers are depicted in films during their first year as they struggle to establish an identity in the classroom and school. As in real life, these cinematic teachers differ from one another in the specific qualities they exhibit. The four styles of teaching are evident—*inventing, knowing, caring,* and *inspiring*—but each style includes two subcategories of experience as shown in Figure 3.3.

Figure 3.3

Styles and Experiences of Teaching

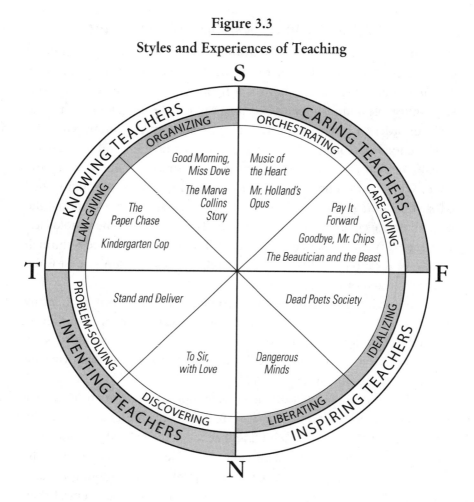

Note: Adapted (with permission) from *Introduction to the CommunicationWheel* (pp. 15–16), by H. L. Thompson, 2000, Watkinsville, GA: Wormhole Publishing. Copyright 2000 by High Performing Systems, Inc.

Images of Inventing Teachers

Inventing teachers are teacher heroes who use strategies in their classrooms that they have personally found get consistently positive results from students. These teachers tend to be realistic, methodical, and structured in their thinking, and are able to defend their practices with logic and reason. Inventing teachers pay little attention to authority, conventional practice, or novelties that happen to be in vogue. Their strategies have proven themselves to be effective for producing tangible results in their particular classroom contexts. The methods that inventing teachers use are varied and ingenious, but they strive almost exclusively to help their students think things through for themselves and understand important concepts.

Examples of inventing teachers are portrayed in *To Sir, with Love* (1967), starring Sidney Poitier, and *Stand and Deliver* (1987), starring Edward James Olmos as real-life teacher Jaime Escalante. Interestingly, the teachers in both these films are male engineers who also happen to be members of ethnic minority groups. In the earlier film, Sidney Poitier plays a native of British Guyana who takes what he believes will be a temporary job teaching in a predominantly white, working-class high school located in the lower east end of London. Although he actively seeks employment as an engineer throughout the film, he increasingly applies his analytical skills to discover ways to connect with his students and to make meaningful the time they spend together in the classroom. By the end of the movie, Poitier's character discovers something important about himself as well—that he has a natural talent for being a teacher. He rejects an opportunity to work as an engineer when an offer finally arrives and decides to return to teaching the following year.

In *Stand and Deliver*, Escalante already has had a successful career as an engineer and becomes a teacher as a way to return something of value to the Latino community. Unlike the teacher portrayed by Poitier, Escalante already understands who he is as a person and what he wants to accomplish. Foremost, he is a problem solver—as an engineer, as a mathematician, and as a teacher. Teaching in an East Los Angeles barrio, Escalante struggles with and successfully solves the very practical problem of making calculus relevant and meaningful to his students so they can pass the Advanced Placement examination, as well as the daunting challenge of overcoming the institutionalized racial prejudice of a national testing company.

Images of Knowing Teachers

Knowing teachers are represented as teachers who hold all students to high standards and consistent rules, without consideration of who the students may be or what prior experiences or disadvantages they may carry into the classroom. True democrats, these teachers expect every student to rise to the academic challenges they confront in the classroom and to be successful. They accept no excuses for failure. Although a knowing teacher's formidable persona may occasionally intimidate and even spark fear in students, gradually building every student's capacity to ultimately triumph over obstacles in a difficult world is the goal that these teachers pursue. Two subcategories of knowing teachers exist—the law-givers and the organizers. Both value conformity to traditional values, understandings, and behaviors.

John Houseman in *The Paper Chase* (1973) and Arnold Schwarzenegger in *Kindergarten Cop* (1990) represent knowing teachers who are both law-givers. As Professor Kingsfield, Houseman greets first-year Harvard law students to his classroom with the memorable pronouncement, "You come in here with a skull full of mush and you leave thinking like a lawyer." In the second film, Schwarzenegger plays an undercover police officer who has trouble relating to kindergarten students until he introduces a benevolent, military-like regimentation, which the youngsters seem to enjoy and other teachers admire. But his main purpose is to bring to justice a murderous drug-dealer who is a threat to one of the students in his kindergarten class.

An early portrayal of a second subcategory of the knowing teacher, the organizer, is found in *Good Morning, Miss Dove*, which was both a best-selling novel (Patton, 1954) and popular movie (1955). Miss Dove is a no-nonsense teacher whose schedule is so regular that people in town gauge their time and set their watches by her appearance on the way to school each morning. We are told that in her elementary geography classroom, "a thing was black or white, right or wrong, polite or rude, simply because Miss Dove said it was" (Patton, 1954, p. 12). While modern readers might be put off by such teacher assertiveness, the author of the book tells us that Miss Dove's methods made her beloved in the town of Liberty

Hill, because her toughening prepared its citizens for the trials they would face in the real world as adults who came of age during World War II.

Award-winning, real-life teacher Marva Collins, portrayed by Cicely Tyson in the television movie *The Marva Collins Story* (1981), represents a more contemporary example of the teacher as an organizer. Highly structured and disciplined, both in personal demeanor and in expectations for others, teachers like Collins have a special knack for using organization in getting students motivated and ready to learn (Collins & Tamarkin, 1990). Marva Collins is said to ask her students, "If you cannot keep one desk orderly, how can you possibly keep the world?" She believes and teaches her students that "if we are not in control of small things, then the larger order of things will not be ours to command" (Marva Collins Seminar, Inc., 2002, p. 3).

Images of Caring Teachers

Caring teachers are portrayed as exhibiting tremendous passion in their classrooms, both for their students and for the subjects that they teach. They are strongly concerned with establishing and maintaining both inner and outer harmony and restoring balance to life. Caring teachers consciously attend to the feeling-tone generated by human interaction in their classrooms and are tuned-in to the emotional needs of every student. They closely monitor the social and emotional dynamics of their classrooms to ensure that all of their students feel important and cared about, learn real skills, gain confidence in their own abilities, and acquire a personal sense of respect and responsibility for themselves and for others. Orchestrators and caregivers are two subcategories of caring teachers that are evident in popular culture depictions.

Orchestrators are illustrated in two fairly recent movies. One example is the film *Music of the Heart* (1999) starring Meryl Streep. Streep portrays a real teacher named Roberta Guaspari who, against tremendous odds, began a successful violin program at a public school in East Harlem. Motivated by intense feeling rather than thinking, orchestrators can be as tough and demanding as organizing teachers. Accused of being "too

harsh" with the children at one point, Streep's character responds by saying, "I'm just trying to teach them discipline. If you want to take a very
difficult instrument, you have to take it seriously, you have to focus, you
have to pay attention." The source of her passionate drive is clarified at the
very end of the film, when she tells her students, who are about to play
with famous violinists at Carnegie Hall, "I would like you all to play from
your heart." A second film that depicts an orchestrating teacher is *Mr.
Holland's Opus* (1995), starring Richard Dreyfuss as a musician who
spends 30 years teaching students to love music and make it a part of their
lives. At the end of the film, the love that he has given is returned. His current and former students perform a complex musical composition that he
has been writing throughout his career, an event that ultimately symbolizes the harmony of his life's work as a teacher.

Teachers who are caregivers, another subcategory of caring teachers,
look after the emotional needs of students and improve the world along
the way by personifying the virtues of compassion and love. An early example of the caregiver is found in Hilton's *Goodbye, Mr. Chips*, classic novel
and Oscar-winning film whose main character emphasizes the importance
of tolerance and balance. Mr. Chipping represents a teacher whose identity
is defined by the consistent care he provides to multiple generations of
students at the same school in England (Pajak, 2002).

Examples of caregivers from contemporary films include teachers in
the comedy *The Beautician and the Beast* (1997), starring Fran Drescher,
and in the drama *Pay It Forward* (2000), with Kevin Spacey. At the start
of *The Beautician and the Beast,* Drescher teaches students who are
preparing to become beauticians. After leading them to safety from a fire
in her classroom, she is hailed as a heroine by the press and hired to tutor
the emotionally starved children of an East European dictator. Her affection liberates the children from their father's tyranny and liberates the
downtrodden citizens of the oppressed country as well. *Pay It Forward*
portrays a teacher who has been physically and emotionally scarred by a
father's cruelty. In response, he works selflessly as a teacher and gives his
students an assignment to make the world a better place.

Images of Inspiring Teachers

Inspiring teachers are depicted as having a flair for making their subjects come alive. They are trendsetters and innovators who are constantly re-inventing themselves. They tend to be creative individuals, even noncon-formists, and they want their teaching to make a statement about what they personally stand for and believe in. They strive to help students think deeply in order to understand themselves and develop unique identities. Inspiring teachers broaden students' horizons about what they can hope to achieve in their lives. They draw out the best in their students by per-suasively and articulately affirming their belief in what students can accomplish. Instead of requiring students to memorize facts, they chal-lenge their students to think deeply about things they encounter in new and different ways.

Inspiring teachers are exemplified by teacher characters in films like *Dead Poets Society* (1989) and *Dangerous Minds* (1995). In the first instance, Robin Williams plays an idealistic English teacher, John Keating, at a conservative college prep school in New England. He encourages his emotionally inhibited students to read poetry for enjoyment and insists that they "seize the day" and live their lives fully in accord with abstract ideals. He urges them to avoid conformity, to think independently, and to experience the world in original ways. Keating's disdain for the thinking function is evident when he ridicules the author of their textbook for asserting that the quality of a poem can be ascertained mathematically by plotting how closely it attains certain goals, and then instructs the stu-dents to tear the offending preface out of their books, leaving only the poetry.

Michelle Pfeiffer is cast as real-life teacher LouAnne Johnson, whose book, *My Posse Don't Do Homework*, inspired the film, *Dangerous Minds*. The teacher in this film also introduces poetry to her class, but her purpose in doing so is to connect with and liberate her inner-city high school students from the limited options imposed on them by society. An ex-marine who wears cowboy boots, her initial rapport with students is established by teaching them hand-to-hand self-defense techniques. This early connection addresses the students' primary concern and struggle for self-preservation in the deadly environment of the streets. Johnson then arms her class with poetry, and inspires the mainly Latino and African-American high school students to take responsibility for their own lives and to rage against the early deaths that drugs and urban street violence promise.

Real-Life Teacher Heroes

These fictional representations of teachers from popular culture are memorable and powerful, because they reflect *archetypes*—that is, images that have existed throughout time. According to Jung, archetypes express energies that arise from deep within our unconscious minds and shape our experience of reality.

But are these archetypes at all meaningful to educators and to education in real life? Are the dramatized qualities of actual teachers like Jaime Escalante, Marva Collins, Roberta Guaspari, and LouAnne Johnson relevant to other teachers whose daily heroic efforts have not been chronicled by Hollywood? I believe that the answer to both questions is undoubtedly "yes!"

For teachers, these archetypes can serve as inner guides that reflect images of the hero that exist within each of us. Recognizing that such images are already a part of us is the first step toward activating their energies and bringing the teacher hero to life in our own classrooms. Knowledge of the archetypes that shape behavior and emotions, both within and outside the classroom, gives teachers the power to increase the range of conscious choices that are available.

Understanding the dominant forces operating within oneself by identifying with a particular narrative increases a teacher's knowledge about his or her unique strengths, abilities, and preferences, and can enrich teachers' relationships with students and colleagues. Such understanding can provide insight into what motivates and frustrates us and our students, and also offers alternatives for finding personal meaning through choices that may open new possibilities.

Expanding our repertoire of archetypes, or at least developing an appreciation for multiple narratives, can enhance and enrich the ways in which we think about what we do in the classroom each day (Reinsmith, 1992). The most capable teachers have access to multiple archetypes and can find fulfillment in a range of manifestations of the teacher role. They are able to act and respond in ways that correspond to the heroic struggles of individual students. In order to help students become heroes or heroines in their own lives (people who make conscious and informed decisions), teachers need to be aware of the powerful forces that operate on an unconscious level and that influence their own behavior and feelings.

Discussion Questions

1. What does teaching mean to you? What about teaching gives you the most satisfaction? How do you know when you have been successful? Compare your answers with those of several colleagues.

2. What books have you read or movies have you seen that depict teachers? Do these examples fit within the *inventing, knowing, caring, and inspiring* experiences?

3. With which type of teacher hero do you most closely identify? Why?

4. How might awareness of the different archetypes of teaching represented in fictional depictions inform teaching practice for a real teacher?

4

Languages, Dialects, and the Clinical Cycle

Jung's concept of psychological functions has recently been adapted and applied to the purpose of better understanding and improving communication within organizations. Thompson (2000) notes that communication is effective only when information and understanding are passed along accurately from a sender to a receiver. Communication problems are likely to arise, he reminds us, when individuals or groups encode or decode messages differently.

What should be especially interesting to theorists and practitioners of clinical supervision, mentoring, and peer coaching is Thompson's (2000) assertion that attending to psychological functions can enhance the quality of interaction between coaches and their clients in all types of organizations. He suggests that the sensing, intuiting, thinking, and feeling functions (S, N, T, and F) can be thought of as four "languages" that people use when communicating. Thompson further proposes that eight communication "dialects" exist (T-N, N-T, S-T, T-S, S-F, F-S, N-F, and F-N) which are determined by whether an individual usually relies more heavily on his or her dominant or auxiliary function to communicate.

Everyone can use both functions, but people tend to rely more heavily on one or the other function to communicate, depending on whether they are introverted or extroverted. People who possess an extroverted nature focus their energy externally, so they use their dominant function when interacting with others. People who are more introverted, in contrast, direct their energy and dominant function inward. Introverts, therefore, rely on their auxiliary function to relate to the external world (Hirsch & Kummerow, 1998).

Somewhat similarly, by adapting Thompson's (2000) model as illustrated in Figure 4.1, we see that the four families of clinical supervision can be understood as representing four languages and eight communication dialects. These correspond closely with the styles and images of teaching that were introduced in Chapter 3.

The Original Clinical Language

The original clinical approaches speak the language of intuition and thinking and give voice to the N-T and T-N communication dialects (see Figure 4.1). These original clinical approaches seek to support teachers in order to increase professional responsibility and openness, as well as enhance their capacity for self-analysis and self-direction. Supervisors are expected to accept every teacher's unique style and help him or her to perfect it by building on existing strengths. Both Goldhammer (1969) and Cogan (1973) describe supervision as a form of democratic inquiry that encourages teachers through dialogue to consider alternatives and choose behaviors rationally according to the probable influence on students.

Despite similarities, the clinical models developed by Goldhammer and Cogan clearly differ in some ways too. Goldhammer (1969) begins his book, for example, by "generating images of what school can be like, particularly in the children's experience" (p. 1). He offers a scathing indictment of the meaninglessness of much that occurs in classrooms and recommends clinical supervision as a way of making instruction more consciously purposeful and responsive to students' needs.

Cogan (1973) grounds his argument for clinical supervision, in contrast, along organizational and professional development lines. He advocates clinical supervision as a practical means for "disseminating and implementing new practices" more effectively and for professionalizing the teaching corps (p. 3). Cogan and Goldhammer also differ in the relative importance each places on objective versus subjective issues. Both

Figure 4.1

Clinical Languages and Dialects

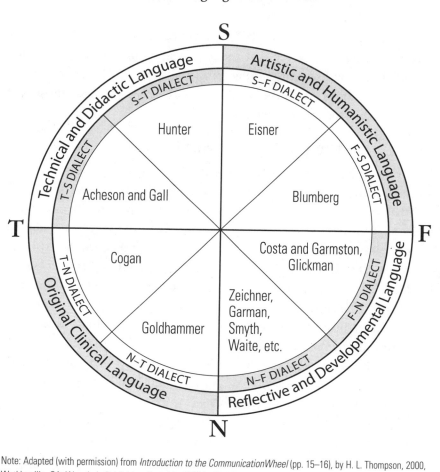

Note: Adapted (with permission) from *Introduction to the CommunicationWheel* (pp. 15–16), by H. L. Thompson, 2000, Watkinsville, GA: Wormhole Publishing. Copyright 2000 by High Performing Systems, Inc.

authors are concerned with observable behaviors, meanings, and the relationship between them as expressed in the teacher's unique teaching style. Cogan urges supervisors to focus attention primarily on teacher behaviors, however, arguing that a change in style will naturally follow: "The proper domain of the clinical supervisor is the classroom behavior of the teacher. That is, the proper subject of supervision is the teacher's classroom behavior, not the teacher as a person" (Cogan, 1973, p. 58).

Goldhammer, on the other hand, advocates consideration of how supervisory processes affect the teacher's "ideas and feelings about himself," beyond "substantive technical learning" (1969, p. 133).

Such differences between the seminal theorists are due to the communication dialect that each expresses in his writings. Although both of these original clinical models contain elements of intuiting and thinking, Goldhammer's view leans closer to conceptual abstraction, while Cogan places greater emphasis on issues of practical application. Goldhammer's approach appears to reflect a communication preference for intuition over thinking, an N-T communication dialect, while Cogan's displays a stronger preference for thinking over intuition, a T-N communication dialect.

According to Keirsey's (1998) classification of psychological temperaments, Goldhammer's perspective parallels the "inventor" and "architect" personality profiles, which draw upon intuition when connecting with others. Cogan's viewpoint is associated with the "fieldmarshal" and "mastermind" categories, which use thinking as the primary channel for communication.

The Technical and Didactic Language

The technical and didactic approaches to clinical supervision advocated by Acheson and Gall and by Hunter plainly give voice to a combination of sensing and thinking (see Figure 4.1). The T-S and S-T dialects speak directly to teachers with law-giving and organizing styles.

Acheson and Gall carry objective analysis to an extreme. Where Goldhammer had five stages and Cogan had eight phases, Acheson and Gall (1980) propose no less than 32 discrete behavioral techniques for classroom observation and conferencing, suggesting an exceptionally heavy reliance on the thinking function. They contrast their *Techniques in the Clinical Supervision of Teachers* with competing texts, noting that other authors "have emphasized theory and research on clinical supervision.

Our book is practical in intent. We emphasize the techniques of clinical supervision, the 'nuts and bolts' of how to work with teachers to help them improve their classroom teaching" (p. xiii).

In comparison, Hunter (1984) draws heavily on her personal experience to inform practice and is concerned with obtaining a complete and accurate record, through "script-taping," of everything that is said and done in the classroom by teachers and students. While every bit as linear and rational as Acheson and Gall, Hunter's version differs in that it requires the clinical supervisor to directly experience and record sensory input, unmediated and unimpeded by observation instruments or mechanical devices. A major advantage of script-taping, she notes, is that "the observer can quickly 'swing' focus from one part of the group to another (something not possible for a camera). This enables an observer to scan and record many parts of the room almost simultaneously" (1984, pp. 185-186).

Thus, although both models express a preference for sensing and thinking, Acheson and Gall place much greater emphasis on the thinking function, or T-S dialect, whereas Hunter emphasizes sensing more heavily than thinking, an S-T dialect. According to Keirsey's (1998) framework, Acheson and Gall's clinical model aligns well with the "inspector" and "supervisor" profiles, while Hunter's clinical approach is consistent with the "crafter" and "promoter" personality configurations.

The Artistic and Humanistic Language

Elliott Eisner (1979) and Arthur Blumberg (1974) propose versions of clinical supervision that contrast sharply with the step-by-step procedures advocated by Acheson and Gall and Hunter. Instead, both Eisner and Blumberg advise supervisors to rely on personal feelings and subjective impressions as guides to clinical practice. These authors emphasize empathy, aesthetic sensitivity, personal credibility, and interpersonal influence instead of control and mechanical application of technique, implying an emphasis on the sensing and feeling functions (see Figure 4.1). They speak the S-F and F-S dialects characteristic of teachers who display the orchestrating and caregiving styles.

Relying on personal sensitivities and experiences, Eisner proposes that an instructional supervisor can become the major instrument through which the classroom and its context are perceived and understood. He believes clinical supervisors should ideally be "connoisseurs" who possess a heightened sensitivity that enables them to perceive what is important yet subtle in classroom behavior and who can eloquently describe its essential expressive value. A close reading of the process that Eisner outlines indicates a very strong emphasis on visual, auditory, and kinesthetic sensing accompanied by a subjective feeling function, or an S-F communication dialect. With Eisner, a combination of heightened sensing and feeling are critical for informing an artistic appreciation of the teaching act: "By artistic I mean using an approach to supervision that relies on the sensitivity, perceptivity, and knowledge of the supervisor as a way of appreciating the significant subtleties occurring in the classroom, and that exploits the expressive, poetic, and often metaphorical potential of language to convey to teachers or to others whose decisions affect what goes on in schools, what has been observed" (1979, p. 59).

Along with Eisner, Blumberg rejects a step-by-step formula. But Blumberg's (1974) model involves feeling as the dominant function coupled with an auxiliary sensing function, resulting in a focus on people and the quality of their interpersonal relationships. As would be expected of an F-S function pair and dialect, Blumberg advises supervisors to concentrate on issues of trust, affection, and influence that he believes create psychological barriers between teachers and supervisors if not addressed. Paralleling the caregiving experience of teaching, he suggests that three conditions must be in place for instructional supervision to be successful: 'the teacher must want help, the supervisor must have the resources to provide the kind of help required or know where the resources may be found, and the interpersonal relationship between a teacher and supervisor must enable the two to give and receive in a mutually satisfactory way" (1980, p. 18).

Applying Keirsey's (1998) classification to the artistic and humanistic approaches aligns Eisner's aesthetic emphasis with the "performer" and "composer" personality configurations. Blumberg's social-emotional focus parallels the "protector" and "provider" profiles.

The Developmental and Reflective Language

Finally, the developmental and reflective approaches, respectively, speak the F-N and N-F communication dialects (see Figure 4.1) of the idealizing and inspiring teaching styles. Both Costa and Garmston's (1994) and Glickman's (1985) versions of clinical supervision place a high premium on feeling and intuition, the F-N dialect, with a focus on empathic understanding and flexible response to teachers' current levels of functioning. Both use empathy and counseling techniques to influence how teachers mentally process information and strongly favor abstract over concrete mental processing. They concentrate primarily on the matter of how supervisors can guide teachers toward conscious understanding and control of their actions in the classroom, as well as when working collectively, to attain desirable learning outcomes for students.

For example, Glickman advocates "instructional supervision that fosters teacher development by promoting greater abstraction, commitment and collective action" (1985, p. 381). Similarly, Costa and Garmston (1994) explain that "cognitive coaching enhances the intellectual capacities of teachers, which in turn produces greater intellectual achievement in students" (p. 6). A major goal of cognitive coaching is "enhancing growth toward *holonomy*," which the authors define as "individuals acting *autonomously* while simultaneously acting *interdependently* with the group" (p. 3). The emphasis on an F-N communication dialect evident in the developmental models is associated with Keirsey's (1998) "teacher" and "counselor" categories.

Advocates of reflective practice, such as Zeichner and Liston (1987), Garman (1986), Waite (1995), and Smyth (1985), also seek to influence cognitive processes, but their position more closely approximates the value-driven N-F dialect. Accordingly, these authors urge supervisors and teachers to question the hierarchical nature of interpersonal relationships in schools, to raise issues of gender, race, and culture to conscious levels

(Waite, 1995), and to challenge the knowledge embodied in the books, curriculum, lessons, and examinations that are part of schooling (Zeichner & Liston, 1987). Teachers and supervisors are encouraged to consider those aspects of classrooms and schools (including their own professional identities) that disempower other educators and debilitate students (Garman, 1986). This potential transformation of schooling is to be fueled by collaborative inquiry and guided by the moral principles of justice and equity (Smyth, 1985). These reflective clinical approaches align closely with Keirsey's "healer" and "champion" personality profiles.

So What?

This entire discussion draws attention to a significant flaw in the way that communication has traditionally been portrayed in the field of supervision. Virtually every model of clinical supervision has imagined communication as being a simple matter of the supervisor telling a teacher what to do, and then *sometimes* listening to what a teacher has to say in response, only if the supervisor believes it is appropriate to do so.

Typically, the experts advise, a balance between listening and telling should be varied according to the supervisor's perception of what a particular teacher "needs." Popular models representing all four families (i.e., Goldhammer, Hunter, Blumberg, and Glickman) have advocated similar ideas for achieving communication with teachers that is balanced in this way, although they differ on the criteria that apply when deciding whether a supervisor should do more of the talking or more of the listening.

Few authors in the field of supervision, if any, have considered the fact that *what a supervisor says may not be what the teacher hears,* and conversely, *what a teacher says may not be what the supervisor hears.* This is not to suggest that the prevailing models of clinical supervision are wrong. Rather, the existing models are only partially correct, because they fail to consider that human beings actively encode and decode information according to their psychological preferences.

Not all communication problems can be traced to differences in psychological type, but communication preferences do serve as filters or refractors that influence our perceptions. These perceptions, distorted somewhat by our personal worldview, ultimately become the realities to which we all respond (See Figure 4.2).

Figure 4.2

Contrasting Views of Information Flow

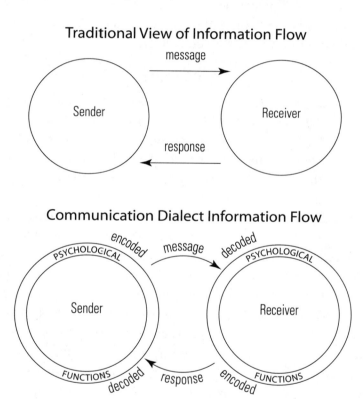

Choosing the right way to communicate with teachers is widely recognized as important. While general consensus exists that care should be taken when selecting a communication style, the experts offer conflicting advice on how to do so.

Goldhammer (1969), writing from an intuiting-thinking point of view (the N-T dialect), for example, cautions supervisors to refrain from being overly direct when working with inexperienced teachers lest they become dependent on the supervisor and fail to develop a personal teaching identity. He advises that experienced veterans can more easily tolerate a supervisor's forthrightness and assimilate into their teaching repertoire what seems appropriate to them, without feeling unduly pressured or intimidated.

In contrast, Hunter (1984), writing from a sensing-thinking perspective (S-T dialect), asserts that being directive is the best way to induct newcomers into the teaching profession, because novices are inexperienced and sorely need the expert advice that a supervisor can provide. Collaborative communication, she believes, should be reserved for teachers who possess the experience and expertise to engage in dialogue with the supervisor on a more equal footing.

Blumberg (1974), expressing a feeling-sensing orientation (F-S dialect), advocates a communication style that combines high-indirect and low-direct behaviors (listening and asking questions with little telling or criticizing) as the most supportive, the most productive, and the most likely to result in high morale when working with all teachers. Glickman (1985), taking a position that emphasizes feeling and intuiting (F-N dialect), argues that a direct style is best suited for a beginning teacher's developmental needs, and an indirect approach is best used to allow more self-direction for teachers who are both highly dedicated and experienced.

Which of these rationales is correct? Each sounds plausible until the other is considered, because every position is consistent within its own internal logic. Yet, each offers advice that is different from the others. Quibbling about the *right* way and the *wrong* way to treat teachers with varying levels of experience and expertise on the basis of the direct and indirect continuum is a waste of time. An understanding of psychological functions and communication dialects allows us to accept a whole range of alternatives that may be appropriate under different sets of circumstances.

A perspective that includes psychological functions as part of the clinical cycle enables us to see that the cognitive processes of the individuals who are involved in the teacher-supervisor relationship make each situation different. While this insight may complicate things a little for both theorists and practitioners of clinical supervision, it also promises a refinement of our understanding and an improvement of our chances for success by moving us beyond the *direct* versus *indirect* communication dilemma.

The basis of a true collegial relationship includes trust and a willingness to share and understand personal meanings and frames of reference. Clinical supervision should provide support for teachers with an aim toward increasing professional responsibility and openness and the capacity for self-analysis and self-direction. By attending carefully to psychological functions, clinical supervisors can recognize and build on teachers' existing strengths. Instead of calling attention to deficits and shortcomings, in other words, clinical supervisors can open alternative paths for teachers to reach their professional goals.

Indeed, tracking teachers according to the supervisor's subjective judgment of their worthiness to be treated as intelligent professional colleagues is as indefensible as the placing of students into different curriculum tracks according to the teacher's perceptions of their academic aptitude. Teachers can be helped to perfect their uniquely personal teaching styles and also round out their repertoires by developing familiarity with styles that include other modes of thinking. Clinical supervisors should initially be willing to accept each teacher's unique style and enter into dialogue with the assumption that the teacher is professionally competent, even though the two of them may experience and respond to the world very differently. Efforts to improve teaching must accommodate multiple viewpoints and understandings or they are otherwise doomed to failure.

Discussion Questions

1. In your own experience, which language or dialect of clinical supervision have you found is used most often in schools? Why might this be true?

2. Which language or dialect of clinical supervision do you personally like the best? What characteristics make it appealing to you?

3. Which language or dialect of clinical supervision do you think would provide the most favorable environment for your own professional growth? Why do you think so?

4. How easy or difficult would it be for you to supervise a *knowing* teacher who displays a sensory-thinking (S-T) function preference? How might you connect interpersonally with such a teacher?

5

Communicating Successfully with *All* Teachers

In earlier chapters we examined the five-stage sequence of the clinical cycle and were introduced to four families of clinical supervision models that have emerged over the past quarter century. Sensing, intuiting, thinking, and feeling, the psychological functions that determine how and why people perceive and process information differently, were explained and shown to parallel the four families of clinical supervision and the multiple ways that teaching can be experienced. Chapter 4 suggested that communication with teachers could be improved by considering the various families and approaches to clinical supervision as representing different languages and dialects. This chapter demonstrates how these ideas can be applied in schools to solve communication problems.

The Clinical Language Circle

In the first chapter, we left principal Flora Seager feeling frustrated about a conference that had gone poorly with a veteran teacher named Sally Taylor. Flora and Sally seem to be locked in a struggle of wills. Sally wants to teach in a way that has been successful for her in the past. Flora prefers that Sally teach in a way that promotes the students' social development.

To help us understand the dynamics at work in the disagreement between Sally and Flora, the *Clinical Language Circle,* adapted from Thompson (2000) is shown in Figure 5.1. The four families of clinical supervision are presented in the outer ring as distinct "languages." The "dialects" comprising these languages express different combinations of sensing (S), feeling (F), intuiting (N), and thinking (T) and are depicted in the middle ring. The inner ring displays the eight styles of teaching (introduced in Chapter 3) that correspond to these communication dialects.

At this point, you should complete the *Clinical Dialect Preference Survey* located in *Appendix A* at the back of this book. If possible, discuss the results with a friend.

Figure 5.1

Clinical Language Circle

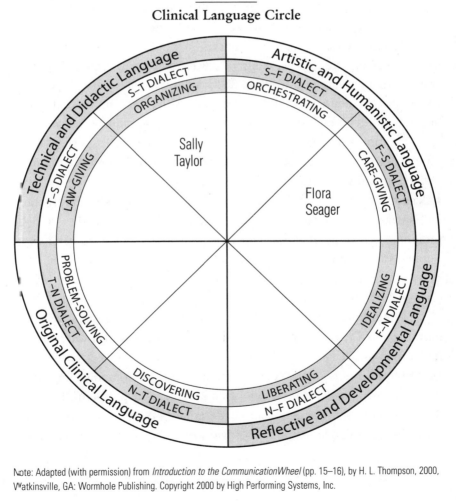

Note: Adapted (with permission) from *Introduction to the CommunicationWheel* (pp. 15–16), by H. L. Thompson, 2000, Watkinsville, GA: Wormhole Publishing. Copyright 2000 by High Performing Systems, Inc.

Sally Taylor's highly structured classroom practice and her comments during the conference suggest a sensory-thinking (S-T) dialect and an organizing style of teaching (see Figure 5.1). Flora Seager's beliefs and comments, in contrast, indicate a feeling-sensing (F-S) dialect and a caregiving style of teaching. Their placement on the *Clinical Language Circle* immediately clarifies the probable source of their conflict. They speak different languages and dialects. They differ, in other words, both in the ways that they gather information and the ways that they process it. The language and dialect each uses when communicating is simply incompatible with the language and dialect spoken by the other.

Existing models of clinical supervision would advise Flora to do two things: 1) do a better job listening to Sally's concerns to establish rapport, and 2) explain the expectations to Sally as directly and clearly as possible. Unfortunately, neither of these strategies will work in this situation, because neither addresses the true cause of the communication problem.

Thompson (2000), who has applied the concept of psychological functions to improve communication in business and other organizational settings, defines communication in the following way: "Communication is a dynamic process of *listening, processing,* and *expressing* information and meaning" (p. 1). The communication cycle is inevitably distorted, he reminds us, by nonverbal behavior, individual interests, values, prior experiences, varying abilities, age, and gender. Differences in processing style, however, are a major source of misunderstanding and conflict in human relationships that we usually overlook.

Communication works best, Thompson (2000) suggests, when both parties speak the same primary language and dialect. If they differ, one or the other must adjust or else communication will break down. Understanding how psychological functions affect communication can be useful for diagnosing the causes of communication problems. Listening for cues about the communication preferences of other people is obviously the key to understanding their view of reality and to making oneself understood by them. Possible solutions to existing problems can be identified and potential problems in supervisory situations may even be avoided entirely by anticipating communication difficulties in advance.

The solution to the problem that Flora and Sally face has little to do with listening more attentively or expressing information more precisely or authoritatively. The central problem in this instance is almost entirely due to the differences in how our two protagonists *process* the information that is spoken and heard. Because of these differences, they can listen and talk to each other for hours, only to reach the conclusion that the other person "just doesn't get it." Flora's use of more directive language in this case, as recommended by many supervision theorists, will prove to be as ineffective as an English-speaking person increasing the volume of her voice in order to be understood when visiting a foreign country.

The prognosis for improving communication in this instance, however, is not hopeless. The two communication dialects exhibited do have the sensing function in common. Sally uses the sensing function to relate externally to the world (S-T), however, while Flora uses sensing as a means of processing information internally (F-S). They may have enough in common to open communication, therefore, if Flora is willing to shift toward the S-F dialect associated with an orchestrating style of teaching and essentially meet Sally halfway. This might mean respecting Sally's close attention to detail and organization, while gradually introducing a broader range of learning outcomes and instructional strategies to her repertoire. If the discrepancy between their dialects and styles of teaching were greater, however, it might be necessary to bring in a third person to serve as a mediator. A peer coach or a specialist from the district office who spoke a dialect that bridged the differences between the teacher and principal would have the best chance of success.

The *Clinical Language Circle* can improve our understanding of group interactions as well. Consider the portfolio review related in the section that follows in terms of the ideas just presented.

The Portfolio Review

Beginning teacher Frank Simons is presenting his end-of-year portfolio to a review team composed of three experienced educators. After reviewing the evidence he presents, the team will make a recommendation about whether he should be granted provisional certification by the state. A positive decision will allow him to teach for two more years, at which time he can apply for permanent certification. A negative decision will mean that Frank must either give up teaching or find another school that will employ him for another year at the beginner level. The members of the review team include: Nancy Thomas, a veteran 6th grade teacher who holds a master's degree in psychology; Tina Sanders, the principal of the elementary school where both Frank and Nancy teach; and Nelson Fogharty, a professor of education from a nearby state university.

Frank is a friendly and personable young man who is obviously interested in pleasing the members of the review committee. He seems to enjoy being the center of attention, smiling broadly as he enthusiastically comments on each component of the portfolio. Frank explains nervously that he had a little difficulty getting the materials together for today. But his many friends, including several of the teachers in the school, kept after him to make sure that the portfolio was finished on time. The material Frank prepared includes samples of work completed by groups of students along with several videotape recordings of lessons that he selected as exemplary. The unit Frank is describing at the moment is one that he designed to help students develop positive self-concepts and social skills. A key lesson involved students in role-playing and sharing information about events in their lives that were personally meaningful to them.

After about 10 minutes, Nelson Fogharty interrupted Frank. "Let me ask you something," he said, "what's the overarching value of all this?"

A little surprised, but not flustered, Frank explained that many 6th graders felt insecure upon entering middle school. He noticed during the second half of the year that students had begun poking fun at classmates who were noticeably different. He described how a particular girl who had grown taller than all the other children was singled out for ridicule and had been given the ironic nickname of "Shorty."

"That's all very interesting," the professor continued, "but can you tell us whether these role-playing activities serve a broader social function?"

"Well," began Frank, a little less certain of himself, "I noticed that this girl that I mentioned had been very verbal and seemed self-assured at the beginning of the school year. After the teasing began, she rarely participated in class discussions and never volunteered to do anything. So, I would say that the social purpose is to help students like her feel better about themselves and also to get other students to be more accepting of individual differences."

"Again, that's all well and good," Dr. Fogharty said. "But I want you to tell me about the big picture. What are the societal implications of the unit you have developed?"

Frank, looking puzzled, was uncharacteristically silent.

Nancy Thomas, who had been assigned to mentor Frank during the year, watched this exchange with interest. She found Frank frustrating to work with, because he almost always had difficulty thinking things through to their logical conclusion without her help. But Nancy had given him feedback on this unit, encouraging him to organize it according to a sequential process of discovery, and therefore felt some ownership. At any rate, she believed that she could lead Frank out of his current difficulty with a little verbal prompting.

"Frank," Nancy began, "do you remember when we identified the objectives for this unit? We talked about how 6th graders were entering a difficult period of adjustment in their lives. As they begin to feel less secure about themselves because of developmental changes, some of them become less tolerant of others and sometimes make fun of students who are different as a way of protecting themselves."

"Yeah. That's right!" said Frank, regaining some of his confidence after recognizing a potential ally in the room. "I remember that now."

"Well that's NOT what I'm talking about," Professor Fogharty responded. "It appears to me," he said, "that you are overlooking entirely the broader social, political, and economic implications of this unit. Specifically, I am referring to discrimination—racial discrimination, gender discrimination, sexual orientation discrimination. Nowhere in your unit are any of these issues explicitly addressed. Your students are certainly at an age when you can introduce issues like economic inequality and political disenfranchisement. I have absolutely no problem with the activities you are using in your classroom, per se. In fact, role-playing can be an especially powerful tool for enlightening people's worldviews. But you're not using the approach to its fullest potential. You seem to be avoiding what should be the main point here. There is absolutely nothing in your portfolio that disrupts your students' underlying assumptions and current ways of thinking about societal issues. You are missing an important opportunity to use cooperative learning and role-playing to focus attention on essential social themes that—"

"Just a minute," Nancy interrupted. "Maybe I wasn't clear enough a moment ago. Frank's unit *is* getting at the psychological process that underlies the kinds of issues that you are talking about. After all, scapegoating and discrimination can originate from inadequacies that individuals and groups feel about themselves. People rely on these behaviors to protect themselves from being singled out and victimized by others. Isn't that what you think Frank?"

Frank just sat there, looking confused and feeling that this meeting was not going as smoothly as he had hoped.

Professor Fogharty, on the other hand, reacted quickly to Nancy's comments. "I am fully aware of the psychological dynamics you just described—Freud's 'narcissism of minor differences' and all of that," Professor Fogharty said. "But I am strongly of the opinion that Frank is not encouraging his students to reflect on matters that relate to the world outside their own classroom. They should not go on believing that they live in an ideal world where everyone always gets along with everyone else."

Not entirely sure whether Professor Fogharty was finished or merely pausing for effect, Frank suddenly found something to say. "Well," he began tentatively, "I guess that having my students get along with each other is exactly what I was trying to accomplish. I want the students in my classroom to feel—"

"Yes," interjected Dr. Fogharty. "You want them to *feel*, to express themselves, to view things from alternative perspectives. But for what purpose? That's what I would like you to tell us."

Just then, Tina Sanders spoke up. "Here it is!" The principal had been busily leafing through various standards documents that each team member had received from the state department of education. "Frank's lessons clearly address several state standards: a 6th grade social studies academic learning standard, 'developing a positive self-concept and social skills,' as well as two standards for teacher performance, 'helping students learn respect for self and others,' and, 'developing a positive classroom climate.' So, what Frank's doing here looks all right to me."

Later, in a private meeting of the review committee, each member expressed reservations about Frank's teaching. Nelson Fogharty again explained that Frank was missing opportunities to have his students reflect on issues of social justice and develop a sense of moral obligation.

Nancy confessed that although she really liked Frank as a person, she had experienced difficulty communicating with him throughout the year and found it frustrating that he seemed unwilling or unable to argue about concepts and ideas. She tried using what the textbooks called a "directive" supervisory approach during their meetings together, but he seemed to have trouble moving beyond asking for advice and seeking her approval.

Tina expressed the opinion, which sounded like a criticism, that Frank was "one of those teachers who just loves kids." "What really worries me," she added, "is whether the students in his class are mastering all the academic content that 6th graders are supposed to be learning."

For a long time, no one said anything, and then everyone began to look concerned.

What Is Going On Here?

Frank, the hero of our story, is obviously caught in a tug-of-war. He knows what he wants to achieve in the classroom, but he has trouble clearly explaining what it is and why he is doing it. He is being pulled in several directions by well-intentioned people who want to be supportive but who have different notions about what Frank ought to do.

This scenario is another example of how educators' conversations often deteriorate, consciously or unconsciously, into opposing factions—individualized learning versus group instruction, cognitive versus affective outcomes, facts versus values, basic skills versus creativity—the list of potential arguments seems endless. The result is that we educators often talk past one another or try unsuccessfully to convince other people that we are right and they are wrong. As was noted in Chapter 1, not only is this bickering counterproductive in the short run, the more dramatic implication is that we prevent ourselves from establishing a professional culture with the uninterrupted narratives we need to inspire us and lead us to greatness.

An analysis of the interaction pattern displayed by the various actors in Frank Simons's ill-fated portfolio review session is presented in Figure 5.2. Based on cues from what people said during the meeting, we can identify the teaching style and communication dialect of each.

The instructional unit that Frank developed and his justification as he presented it to the panel suggest that he possesses a caregiving style of teaching, and speaks an F-S (feeling-sensing) communication dialect. Frank is obviously very much concerned with the personal adjustment and social well being of the students in his classroom. He is proud of the fact that he has established a positive climate where students' feelings are respected. But he has difficulty connecting his practice to more abstract values and ideas.

Nancy Thomas, the mentor teacher, seems to display a discovering style of teaching. Her analytical approach to the meeting, her ease with theoretical concepts, and her use of Socratic questioning during the meeting also imply an N-T (intuiting-thinking) dialect. Nancy's distance from

Figure 5.2

Clinical Language Circle 2

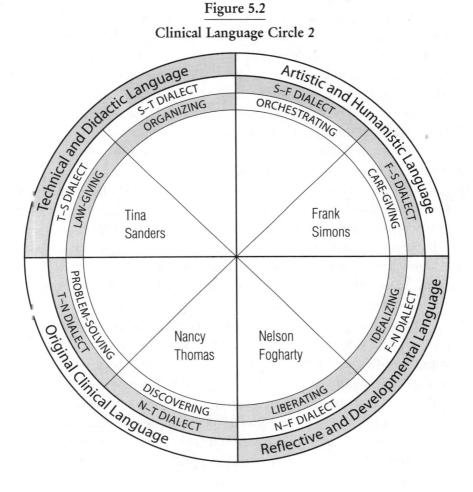

Note: Adapted (with permission) from *Introduction to the CommunicationWheel* (pp. 15–16), by H. L. Thompson, 2000, Watkinsville, GA: Wormhole Publishing. Copyright 2000 by High Performing Systems, Inc.

Frank on the *Clinical Language Circle* (see Figure 5.2) explains why she found working with Frank so difficult. Because of how she processes information, Nancy's commitment to seeing Frank succeed is based essentially on the intellectual challenge he presents. In other words, she does not want to be proven wrong.

The principal, Tina Sanders, focuses exclusively on student learning outcomes and whether performance standards are being met. Tina appears to display a law-giving style of teaching in her concern with external indicators of success and to speak a T-S (thinking-sensing) dialect. Although she shares a sensing function with Frank, she is not well equipped to deal with feelings, which represents the primary way that Frank relates to the external world.

Finally, Professor Fogharty's insistent appeal for broader purposes that relate to moral, social, and political matters suggests an N-F (intuiting-feeling) dialect characteristic of a liberating teaching style. He approaches issues from an abstract level and, in that sense, is most compatible with Nancy Thomas. However, the difference in their auxiliary functions (feeling versus thinking) does provide a cause for spirited debate. Communication between Nelson and the principal, Tina Sanders, is likely to be more difficult because they perceive and process information entirely differently (N-F versus T-S).

Interestingly, Professor Fogharty is the member of the portfolio review panel who has the best chance of communicating successfully with Frank. Despite his confrontational manner, Nelson is closer to Frank on the *Clinical Language Circle* than any other team member (see Figure 5.2). In order to improve communication with Frank, however, Nelson should seek to employ an F-N dialect, rather than the N-F communication dialect that comes naturally to him, and strive to become a better listener.

Practically, this would mean that the professor should draw on the rationale and strategies of clinical supervision recommended by authors like Costa and Garmston (1994) and Glickman (1985). These developmental models of clinical supervision most directly address the idealizing style of teaching. By drawing on developmental coaching behaviors, which express the F-N dialect, Professor Fogharty will more closely approximate Frank's F-S style of teaching and communicating. Doing so will provide an opportunity for Frank to grow beyond the caregiving style he currently exhibits, in the direction of an idealizing style of teaching.

This scenario sheds light on another contemporary issue, as well—shaping the content of communication with teachers on the basis of the goals that a supervisor hopes to accomplish. Several authors writing from a developmental/reflective perspective have independently recommended that a supervisor's practice should be guided by whether the object is to improve a teacher's technical competence, conceptual understanding, or sensitivity to ethical issues (e.g., Grimmett, 1989; Zeichner & Liston, 1996). In each instance, a hierarchy of goals favoring moral sensitivity over technical competence, with conceptual understanding between them, is explicitly stated.

A view of clinical supervision that considers psychological functions suggests that this hierarchy of goals is essentially arbitrary, except from the perspective of those like Professor Fogharty, who favor intuition and feeling as ways of perceiving and evaluating reality. A supervisor with a sensing-thinking combination, like Tina Sanders, will probably consider an idealistic and well-intentioned teacher who lacks the skills needed to help students learn more problematic than a motivated and technically proficient teacher who expresses little concern for principles of social justice.

A view informed by psychological functions further suggests that in addition to technical (S-T), conceptual (N-T), and moral (N-F) considerations, a relational (S-F) dimension of growth is also possible, desirable, and seriously worth considering as an outcome of both instruction and supervision. Without questioning the value of technical skills, abstract thinking, or moral commitment, in other words, the legitimacy and importance of developing the sensing-feeling functions for students, teachers, and supervisors becomes evident.

Multiple Applications

The *Clinical Language Circle* has a variety of practical applications in schools, and particularly for clinical supervisory relationships, that are worth noting. The following represent examples of the major applications.

• *Assigning mentors and peer coaches.* Beginning teachers will find it easier to talk openly with a mentor or peer coach who has a teaching style and speaks a dialect that is close to their own. A perfect match of psychological functions is not necessary and may not provide the best environment for growth. A small discrepancy, as in the case of Frank Simons and Nelson Fogharty, may be optimal because the gap requires both the teacher and the supervisor to grow toward one another.

• *Selecting team members.* A clinical supervision team, or any team of educators working together, can benefit from having a variety of teaching styles and clinical languages represented. Such diversity is likely to promote more creative problem solving and will ensure that multiple voices representing a range of teaching experiences get heard.

• *Improving communication.* Existing pairs or teams of educators who are involved in clinical cycles, or who have other duties to perform collectively, can improve their performance by analyzing communication patterns. Open discussion of similarities and differences in the styles, dialects, and languages can build trust and improve communication by increasing awareness of information processing challenges that may exist.

• *Resolving conflicts.* Pairs or teams of educators who work together can identify areas where miscommunication and misunderstanding are most likely to occur. By becoming aware of different information processing orientations, communication between and among members will improve as everyone learns to adjust their own styles to accommodate the preferences of others. Good listening skills and the clarity of spoken messages, of course, continue to be important.

• *Identifying mediators.* Occasionally it may be necessary to bring in a third party to resolve differences and facilitate communication when information processing differences are too great. The third party can be selected by using the *Clinical Language Circle* to ensure that he or she can successfully fill the role of mediator or interpreter for people who speak different clinical languages.

• *Professional development.* Teacher mentors, peer coaches, instructional supervisors, and principals can use the *Clinical Language Circle* to better understand their personal style of teaching, preferred dialect, and supervisory language in order to identify directions for their own professional growth. The more proficient clinical supervisors become with multiple languages and dialects, the more flexibility they achieve, and the more successful they will become in supporting a wider range of teaching styles.

Discussion Questions

1. Locate yourself and a friend or colleague on the Clinical Language Circle and discuss how well you are likely to work together. What strengths will you each bring to the relationship? What are some blind spots that will have to be contended with? How might you compensate for those blind spots?

2. If you were invited as a peer coach to mediate between Flora Seager and Sally Taylor, how would you prepare for that assignment? What difficulties would you anticipate?

3. Imagine that you are Professor Fogharty and that you will be working with Frank Simons, who has had the good fortune of being rehired provisionally for another year. How will you prepare? What difficulties do you anticipate?

4. Why do you think the sensing-feeling dimension of professional growth for teachers has been overlooked by most experts in the field of supervision? What contributions might a teacher with a strong sensing-feeling orientation make to a classroom and school?

Speaking the Languages and Dialects

6

The clinical cycle is being used today more often than ever before by teachers themselves, in roles as mentors and peer coaches, to improve instruction in classrooms and to socialize beginning teachers into the profession. Although this trend suggests a positive movement toward a less hierarchical collegial responsibility for the quality of teaching in schools, an important element is still missing—acceptance of the fact that teachers differ in the ways that they view reality and make decisions. As a result, clinical supervision goes on in the same old way, completely ignoring differences in teaching styles. What the profession really needs is a *new vision* for clinical supervision. This new vision should include the following characteristics:

• Teaching styles are recognized as the proper starting point for planning professional growth.

• Diagnosis is used to make the clinical cycle more responsive to teachers' real learning needs.

• Multiple teaching and information processing styles are honored.

• Progress is measured by individual teacher development.

• Multiple supervisory languages and dialects are spoken to accommodate differences among teachers.

• Clinical supervisors flexibly provide differentiated learning environments that are appropriate for every teacher's professional growth.

This chapter offers specific ideas for bringing this new vision of clinical supervision to reality. Suggestions are made for tailoring the clinical cycle to better meet the needs of *inventing, knowing, caring,* and *inspiring* teachers, as well as tips for speaking the dialects that can help improve communication. An overview of how the clinical cycle can be differentiated is provided in Figure 6.1.

Before beginning the clinical cycle, both the teacher's and the clinical supervisor's style preferences should be identified. After a clinical supervisor becomes thoroughly familiar with the concept of psychological functions and their manifestation in behavior and language, he or she will be able to informally assess a teacher's style and preferred dialect through observation and attentive listening. The three questions that were introduced in Chapter 3 concerning the meaning of teaching, satisfaction, and success can provide a context for a conversation wherein an informal assessment can be made.

A more formal written assessment, however, is useful for verifying the supervisor's initial impressions. A survey can also serve as a starting point for a discussion about teaching styles and clinical languages. The instrument included in Appendix A at the end of this volume provides a fairly accurate assessment of style, especially with respect to the process of the clinical cycle. Alternative or supplementary instruments include the surveys found in Champagne and Hogan (1995) and Silver, Strong, and Perini (2000). The most accurate instruments for determining psychological functions, along with other measures related to psychological type, are the Keirsey Temperament Sorter (Keirsey, 1998) and the Myers-Briggs Type Indicator (1996). Except for the Myers-Briggs, all of these are self-scoring instruments.

The Clinical Cycle for Inventing Teachers

Inventing teachers rely most strongly on intuition and thinking to understand the world around them, including their work as teachers. The instructional goal that most often guides their classroom efforts is to help students collect and examine data and learn to reach logical conclusions.

Figure 6.1
Differentiating the Clinical Cycle

	Clinical Cycle for Inventing Teachers (N-T or T-N)	Clinical Cycle for Knowing Teachers (S-T or T-S)	Clinical Cycle for Caring Teachers (S-F or F-S)	Clinical Cycle for Inspiring Teachers (N-F or F-N)
Stage 1 Pre-Observation Conference	Pose hypotheses about possible relationships between teacher behaviors and student behaviors.	Establish a clear understanding of what effective teaching looks like and how it can be documented with evidence.	Develop trust and a positive climate that will contribute to collaboration and mutual learning.	Share, discuss, and reflect upon personal values and beliefs about teaching and its purposes.
Stage 2 Observation	Make a written or electronic record of everything that is said and done by the teacher and the students.	Document the presence and the absence of teacher and student behaviors according to a preselected focus.	Capture the feeling-tone of the classroom by richly describing the social and emotional qualities of the human interaction.	Record a rich illustrative narrative description of what is seen and heard, including impressions that are evoked.
Stage 3 Analysis and Strategy	Look for patterns of teacher and student behavior and organize them in a logical order.	Identify patterns of data that are consistent with the agreed-upon definition of effective teaching.	Look for concrete examples of success that will build the teacher's confidence and reinforce good practices.	Examine the data for evidence of higher-order thinking and dedication to moral principles.
Stage 4 Postobservation Conference	Discuss and even debate meanings of events as colleagues, but avoid directly telling the teacher what to do.	Highlight data that illustrate the presence or absence of desired teacher and student behaviors.	Demonstrate empathy, accept feelings, praise achievements, and avoid being evaluative.	Reflect on the personal, social, and political implications of the lesson and examine taken-for-granted assumptions, values, and beliefs.
Stage 5 Postconference Analysis	Review the previous four stages and analyze each to determine its contribution to the success of the clinical cycle.	Review the previous four stages to ensure that each was completed correctly and as planned.	Review the previous four stages to make certain that trust and a positive climate for learning have not been compromised.	Review the previous four stages to ensure that consistency exists between espoused values and enacted behaviors.

These teachers are likely to rely heavily on inquiry or discovery methods of instruction in their classrooms. They tend to prefer professional development that focuses on hypothesis testing, feedback on student learning, feedback on teacher questions, at-task analysis, and action research. The original clinical approaches of Goldhammer (1969) and Cogan (1973) provide a clinical language that most closely matches the learning style of inventing teachers.

Stage 1—Pre-Observation Conferences with Inventing Teachers:

Pose hypotheses about possible relationships between teacher behaviors and student behaviors.

Planning is something that inventing teachers enjoy doing and they will appreciate being given an opportunity to think a lesson through aloud. The supervisor can rely on an indirect or Socratic line of questioning to allow the teacher to draw answers from his or her own experience. Inventing teachers are confident in their area of specialization. They are comfortable dealing with theories and concepts, and are adept at identifying and proposing relationships between ideas. Although they are comfortable with abstractions, inventing teachers prefer organization and coherent structure in their classrooms. Posing hypotheses about cause-and-effect relationships between teacher behaviors and student behaviors will come naturally to them and will be a motivating feature of the clinical supervision cycle. Lesson plans that result from the pre-observation conference will be rationally arranged within a broader conceptual framework.

Stage 2—Observation of Inventing Teachers:

Make a written or electronic record of everything that is said and done by the teacher and the students.

Given an opportunity to craft a plan for the lesson during the pre-observation conference, inventing teachers will execute the plan enthusiastically and will take pride in displaying their ability to lead students to logical conclusions. They are likely to anticipate student questions, as well as points during the lesson where problems might arise, but they also possess creative flexibility and are able to capitalize on unanticipated occurrences. Students may be actively involved, as in a lab activity, or the lesson may take the form of a structured discussion or debate. In any case, lessons will be organized rationally, leading students inductively from an examination of evidence toward a discovery of concepts and generalizations, or deductively by applying principles and facts in order to reach logical conclusions.

Stage 3—Analysis and Strategy for Inventing Teachers:

Look for patterns of teacher and student behavior and organize them in a logical order.
Data analysis and hypothesis testing come naturally to inventing teachers, so supervisors may want to involve the teacher in the discovery process. These teachers are likely to view the opportunity to participate in this stage as an interesting problem-solving challenge. They will be very adept at finding patterns in the data presented to them.

Stage 4—Postobservation Conferences with Inventing Teachers:

Discuss and even debate meanings of events as colleagues, but avoid directly telling the teacher what to do.
The inventing teachers will probably exhibit considerable independence during the conference because the process of discovery will fascinate them. They are likely to anticipate conclusions and recommendations that the supervisor has prepared in advance. Progress during the conference can be facilitated by asking open-ended questions and employing Socratic questioning.

Stage 5—Postconference Analysis for Inventing Teachers:

Review the previous four stages and analyze each to determine its contribution to the success of the clinical supervision cycle.
Keep in mind that the stages of the clinical cycle provide a logical process for solving problems of classroom practice.

Speaking the Discovering (N-T) Dialect

Teachers whose communication dialect is consistent with an N-T function pair are likely to be analytical, adaptable, and full of ideas. When working with teachers who fit this profile, a clinical supervisor ought to:

• Be ready to answer questions that relate to the big picture.

• Draw out teacher creativity by emphasizing the problem-solving aspect of clinical supervision and future possibilities.

• Remain flexible and open to free-flowing insights and ideas proposed by the teacher.

• Keep the discussion grounded in the data and its practical implications.

• Allow plenty of time for teachers to think things through, because they will want to consider every facet of a new idea before implementing it.

Speaking the Problem-Solving (T-N) Dialect

Teachers who display a T-N communication preference, where thinking is dominant over intuition, are organized and purposeful in their instruction, and logical and strategic in their thinking. When working with teachers who display this profile it is especially important to:

• Be well prepared in advance and organized in your presentation.

• Be ready for some skeptical questions and a complex grasp of reality.

• Build on the teacher's capacity for innovative thinking and desire to improve.

• Focus on cause-and-effect relationships between events, and the creative qualities of the teacher's ideas.

• Get to the point quickly, then be ready to spend time debating specific interpretations.

• Rely on logical reasoning, both to maintain credibility and to establish the legitimacy of your interpretations of the data.

The Clinical Cycle for Knowing Teachers

Knowing teachers rely most heavily on the sensing and thinking functions to understand the world around them, including their work as teachers. The instructional goal that most often guides their classroom efforts is to help students acquire knowledge and skills, and learn to organize information. These teachers are likely to rely heavily on direct instruction in their classrooms. They prefer professional development that focuses on skill training, category checklists, and feedback on fidelity of teacher behavior to performance standards. The technical approach of Acheson and Gall (1980) and the didactic approach suggested by Hunter (1984), as well as the work of Harris and Hill (1982) and Danielson (1996), provide a language that most closely matches the learning style of knowing teachers.

Stage 1—Pre-Observation Conferences with Knowing Teachers:

Establish a clear understanding of what effective teaching looks like and how it can be documented with evidence.

Knowing teachers will be eager to describe what they intend to do in great detail. Explaining things to other people is something that they enjoy doing. The supervisor can ask specific questions about what will happen during the lesson to be observed and expect to receive clear and straightforward answers. These teachers are likely to have a solid grasp of the subjects that they teach and are confident about the methods of instruction that they employ. They are comfortable dealing with facts and details, and are good at organizing information sequentially and hierarchically. Because they prefer dealing with concrete reality, knowing teachers emphasize facts and knowledge of concepts in their lessons. Their instruction tends to be structured and focused on objectives, with right and wrong answers clearly delineated. Having an opportunity to describe and explain in detail what they are going to do in the classroom will be motivating at this stage of the clinical cycle. Lesson plans that result from the pre-observation conference will be logically arranged within a specified step-by-step structure.

Stage 2—Observation of Knowing Teachers:

Document the presence and the absence of teacher and student behaviors according to a preselected focus.
By participating in the selection of data to be recorded, knowing teachers will want to ensure that everything agreed upon at the pre-observation conference is carried out. They are likely to follow the lesson plan point by point, leaving nothing to chance. Students' attention may be monitored through occasional questions and answers, while the teacher directs all activity toward a specific preselected learning objective. Facts to be mastered are usually organized according to conceptual categories determined by the teacher in advance.

Stage 3—Analysis and Strategy for Knowing Teachers:

Identify patterns of data that are consistent with the agreed-upon definition of effective teaching.
Supervisors should match the data against the criteria of performance agreed upon in advance. Finding out whether or not the data show that the lesson was conducted as originally planned will be of primary interest to knowing teachers. The supervisor's presentation of findings should be precise and logically organized or the knowing teacher will not find it credible.

Stage 4—Postobservation Conferences with Knowing Teachers:

Highlight data that illustrate the presence or absence of desired teacher and student behaviors.
The post observation conference is likely to be viewed by knowing teachers as an opportunity to have their capability confirmed. They will

probably challenge the supervisor on matters of fact, especially if the supervisor appears to be uncertain or unprepared. Supervisors can facilitate progress during the conference by being direct, descriptive, and unequivocal.

Stage 5—Postconference Analysis for Knowing Teachers:

Review the previous four stages to ensure that each was completed correctly and as planned.
Keep in mind that the stages of the clinical cycle can be a reliable mechanism for self-correction.

Speaking the Law-Giving (T-S) Dialect

Teachers who rely on a T-S communication dialect, where thinking is dominant over sensing, tend to be structured, conservative, and businesslike in their demeanor. Their thinking is logical, practical, and literal. Their instruction is likely to focus heavily on facts and details, and their classroom routines are often meticulously planned. When working with these teachers, clinical supervisors should:

• Be well prepared with facts and ready to present the data and interpretations in a logical sequence.

• Emphasize the practical benefits of clinical supervision.

• Rely on analysis and reason to persuade.

• Be clear about expectations and firm about interpretations, because these teachers are likely to have their own agendas clearly in mind.

• Allow the teacher time to change and make adjustments to established routines.

Speaking the Organizing (S-T) Dialect

Teachers with a sensing-thinking communication preference are very observant and conscious of the immediate situation. They tend to be concrete, realistic, and analytic in their thinking. Their instruction is likely to be experientially active, with an emphasis on practical skills and facts. When working with teachers who display an S-T preference, one should:

• Be friendly yet maintain some professional distance.
• Focus on the functional benefits of getting a problem solved.
• Be clear, direct, and to the point.
• Appeal to observable facts and logic to support interpretations.
• Allow the conference agenda to move forward fairly quickly, but be prepared to spend time listening to the teacher's concerns.
• Provide time for the teacher to think through new ideas and the implications of changing his or her established way of doing things.

The Clinical Cycle for Caring Teachers

Caring teachers rely most heavily on the sensing and feeling functions to understand the world around them, including their work as teachers. The instructional goal that most often guides their classroom efforts is to help students understand and respect themselves, and cooperate with others. These teachers are likely to employ instructional activities that encourage students to learn in groups. They tend to prefer professional development that involves study groups, peer coaching, teacher networks, feedback on climate and ambience, movement patterns, and anecdotal records of classroom events. The artistic approach advocated by Eisner (1979) and the humanistic approach of Blumberg (1974) provide a language that most closely matches the learning style of caring teachers.

Stage 1—Pre-Observation Conferences with Caring Teachers:

Develop trust and a positive climate that will contribute to collaboration and mutual learning.
Caring teachers are naturally warm and friendly. Interpersonal relationships are very important to them and they are very comfortable with face-to-face communication. It is essential to establish a strong personal bond from the very beginning, so special attention should be given to eye contact and active listening. It is also good practice for the clinical supervisor to follow social conventions such as saying "good afternoon" and to avoid any behavior or language that might be interpreted as disrespectful

toward the teacher or other people. Focus the conversation on the influence that teaching has on the well-being of students. Caring teachers may need assistance thinking through a detailed lesson plan beyond the routines that they already have in place. Explicitly describe the stages of the clinical cycle that will follow and check to be sure that the teacher understands what is expected to happen.

Stage 2—Observation of Caring Teachers:

Capture the feeling-tone of the classroom by richly describing the social and emotional qualities of the human interaction.

Lessons planned by caring teachers typically include routines that ensure student involvement and a shared sense of belonging. Instructional processes may appear to take precedence over the mastery of content, when in fact significant student learning is occurring beneath the surface. When gathering data, the observer should record what is happening in rich detail, especially between the teacher and students, and within groups of students in the classroom. Then look for patterns of interaction, especially those that provide evidence of positive outcomes.

Stage 3—Analysis and Strategy for Caring Teachers:

Look for concrete examples of success that will build the teacher's confidence and reinforce good practices.

Getting a strong sense of what actually happened during the lesson will be of great interest to caring teachers. They will appreciate a descriptive narrative that captures the subtle details of life in their classroom more than objective forms of data, particularly numerical representations. When analyzing the data, make explicit connections between observed events and the feeling tone or climate of the classroom, as well as to learning outcomes for students.

Stage 4—Postobservation Conferences with Caring Teachers:

Demonstrate empathy, accept feelings, praise achievements, and avoid being evaluative.

Presenting the data from the observation is a good way to begin. Build on evidence of success initially and link student behaviors with particular events whenever possible. Be specific with regard to data, interpretations, and suggestions, and be ready to recommend a series of steps to be taken for improvement. Remain aware that caring teachers can be very sensitive, however, and that their feelings are easily hurt. Offer generous and sincere praise for good work, honor all agreements, and be sure to follow-up on any promises that are made. These teachers are open to suggestions, but may have difficulty making changes. They can benefit from observing other teachers and getting feedback from them.

Stage 5—Postconference Analysis for Caring Teachers:

Review the previous four stages to ensure that trust and a positive climate for learning have not been compromised.
Keep in mind that the stages of the clinical cycle offer a process for encouraging trust, collegial dialogue, and mutual understanding.

Speaking the Orchestrating (S-F) Dialect

Teachers who display a sensing-feeling dialect are personable and often fun-loving. They are sensitive and caring toward other people, especially their students. Their teaching is exciting and spontaneous and may even exhibit a certain playfulness. When communicating with teachers who exhibit an S-F function pairing, supervisors should:

• Be collegial and generally straightforward when presenting data, but avoid seeming to be insensitive or confrontational.

• Draw out and build on the teacher's warmth, spontaneity, and energy.

• Emphasize the immediate practical benefits of improving instruction for students.

• Respond promptly to the teacher's request for resources or assistance.

Speaking the Caregiving (F-S) Dialect

Teachers for whom feeling predominates over sensing are very conscientious and concerned with the well-being of others. They are friendly and gentle, but hold strong personal convictions and act upon them. These teachers are caring and highly sensitive to their students' personal well-being. Their instruction provides students with both social and emotional support. Supervisors should take special care to:

- Build a personal rapport with the teacher by demonstrating respect for them as a person.
- Be on time for the observation and conference.
- Maintain good eye contact and listen attentively.
- Emphasize the importance of students and their feelings of efficacy.

The Clinical Cycle for Inspiring Teachers

Inspiring teachers rely most heavily on the intuition and feeling functions to understand the world around them, including their work as teachers. The instructional goal that most often guides their classroom effort is to help students express personal values and develop a sense of vitality and purpose in life. These teachers are likely to employ creative approaches in the classroom that challenge students to reflect on personal values and social issues. They prefer professional development that involves journaling, reflection, verbal flow, and feedback on teacher sensitivity to student differences. The developmental approaches of Glickman (1985) and Costa and Garmston (1994), and the reflective approaches of Garman (1986), Smyth (1985), Waite (1995), and Zeichner and Liston (1996) offer a clinical language that most closely matches the learning style of inspiring teachers.

Stage 1—Pre-Observation Conferences with Inspiring Teachers:

Share, discuss, and reflect upon personal values and beliefs about teaching and its purposes.

Inspiring teachers enjoy face-to-face communication, but they prefer to converse about abstractions instead of details. In order to build rapport, be prepared to talk about philosophy, values, and convictions initially, but be ready to focus the discussion on the task of finding alternative solutions to real problems. Emphasize the teacher's contribution to students and society, and the opportunities that creative ideas can make possible. Unleash the teacher's imagination by mirroring his or her passion and encourage his or her involvement in brainstorming areas for improvement and innovative solutions. The ideas that are generated may have to be narrowed down to a manageable number. Because inspiring teachers rely heavily on spontaneity in the classroom and believe in its value, it may be difficult to get more than a rough outline of the lesson that will be taught.

Stage 2—Observation of Inspiring Teachers:

Record a rich and illustrative narrative description of what is seen and heard, including subjective impressions that are evoked.

Be prepared for the possibility of observing a lesson that is much different from what you expected. Inspiring teachers value spontaneity and innovation so highly that they may not be aware that they have made changes to the plan that has been agreed upon. They may even expect to be praised for their initiative and originality for doing something unexpected. Indeed, the lesson is likely to be very creative and exhibit a high degree of student participation and direction. The lesson may appear to take on a life of its own at times, as the teacher takes advantage of learning opportunities that unexpectedly arise. Look for evidence of recurring themes that relate to philosophical, social, or ethical issues and purposes that were discussed during the pre-observation conference.

Stage 3—Analysis and Strategy for Inspiring Teachers:

Examine the data for evidence of higher-order thinking and dedication to moral principles.

Look for examples of consistency and discrepancy between real behaviors and ideals espoused during the pre-observation conference. Inspiring teachers are typically very good at recognizing patterns, so allowing them to suggest alternative ways of interpreting the data can be beneficial. Plan to begin the conference by presenting the overarching issues first and allow frequent opportunities for the teacher to respond.

Stage 4—Postobservation Conferences with Inspiring Teachers:

Reflect on the personal, social, political, and economic implications of the lesson and examine taken-for-granted assumptions, values, and beliefs.

Inspiring teachers are likely to display considerable independence during the conference. Staying grounded in the data is important, but relate it to values and ideals at every opportunity to ensure that they perceive it as relevant. Otherwise, the teacher will soon find the details tedious and will try to move the conversation in another direction. Be aware of the necessity to avoid serious confrontation that might move the conference off track. Inspiring teachers delight in focusing on the future, so be prepared to move quickly into the identification of innovative solutions and remain open to unusual proposals. Encourage the teacher to work toward achieving his or her high ideals and to bring his or her personal values into reality.

Stage 5—Postconference Analysis for Inspiring Teachers:

Review the previous four stages to ensure that consistency exists between espoused values and enacted behaviors.

Keep in mind that the stages of the clinical cycle represent a process for making teaching and learning more meaningful.

Speaking the Idealizing (N-F) Dialect

Teachers whose intuition guides their feelings are both curious about new possibilities and passionate about their personal ideals. They are likely to be nonconformists, easily bored with facts and details, comfortable talking about values and convictions, and very open to change. Their instruction in the classroom is likely to be dramatic, energetic, imaginative, and fast-paced. Supervisors should:

    • Be ready to spend time building rapport by sharing personal values and convictions.

• Avoid getting into a conflict over values by staying relaxed, open-minded, and tolerant.

• Move quickly from the data to the need for innovative solutions to real problems.

• Emphasize the benefits that testing their assumptions will have for students.

Speaking the Liberating (F-N) Dialect

Individuals who exhibit an F-N psychological profile are empathic, hold strong beliefs, and want to make their own decisions. They are clear communicators and decisive in their actions. The instruction of teachers who display an F-N style is highly creative, and emphasizes personal development, values, and understanding of abstract ideas. When working with teachers who fit this profile, one should:

• Be tactful and show respect for the personal feelings and values espoused by these teachers.

• Be ready for deep and far-ranging philosophical discussions.

• Encourage their natural creativity and appeal to their desire to encourage growth and development in their students and in themselves.

• Show support for their decisions and encourage them to put their good intentions into action.

• Emphasize broad future-oriented goals more than narrowly specific outcomes in the present.

Some Words of Caution and Clarification

The advice presented in this chapter is not intended and should never be used to pigeonhole teachers into ironclad stereotypes. Personally, I believe that the practice of tracking teachers according to the supervisor's subjective perception of their ability is as indefensible as the tracking of students.

In truth, even the most structured *knowing* teacher is capable of exhibiting creativity, and the most flexible *inspiring* teacher can become entrenched in a relentlessly predictable pattern of behavior. The clinical coach should be just as sensitive to the feelings of *inventing* teachers as they are to *caring* teachers, and ought to remember that the latter are every bit as capable of grappling with complex intellectual concepts as are the former.

The ideas offered in this chapter relate to psychological *preferences* that we all possess for perceiving and processing information. The suggestions provided are intended solely as practical ideas for improving human understanding by focusing the attention of clinical coaches on the differences that exist among different types of teachers, without implying that any particular type is inherently better than any other. Above all, it is essential that clinical coaches get to know the teachers with whom they work as people. Consideration of individual styles should then be used to provide teachers with alternative paths for improving their practice.

As a clinical coach, your responsibility is to improve the instruction in the classrooms of teachers with whom you work. The more tools that you have at your disposal, the more successful you are likely to be. To help yourself think through how you might communicate more effectively with *inventing, knowing, caring,* and *inspiring* teachers, complete the worksheets provided in *Appendix B* at the back of this book.

Discussion Questions

1. Are the suggestions for improving communication that are presented in this chapter likely to make the clinical cycle more successful? Why or why not?

2. What drawbacks, if any, might be anticipated from using the different languages and dialects during the clinical cycle?

3. How would awareness of the various languages and dialects improve the functioning of teams of teachers as they work together?

4. Share your responses to the worksheets in Appendix B with a colleague. Where do you have the most opportunity to grow?

7

Developing an Integrated Style

The universal popularity of the hero's quest in myth and popular fiction is due to the fact that the story describes a process of psychological maturation, an experience with which we all can identify. Maturation involves attaining wholeness and integrity through increased awareness of our conscious and unconscious worlds. Becoming a successful teacher, like becoming a hero, requires a great deal of hard work combined with generous portions of "cleverness, help, luck, and perseverance" (Hopcke, 1999).

Although any one of the experiences of teaching—*inventing, knowing, caring,* or *inspiring*—can serve as a useful guide to practice for a teacher, all of these paths must be traced if a teacher is to become truly effective. A teacher hero is different from any other hero, after all, because during the journey toward defining one's own identity, a teacher encounters and influences the questing heroes of future generations. Each student that a teacher meets in the classroom requires different things at different times—explanations and reliable ways of thinking, high standards and self-confidence, nurturing care and emotional support, inspiration and values—and a teacher ought to be ready to provide them all.

Hanson and Silver (1998) go so far as to suggest that teachers who rely exclusively on one or two functions are neither effective nor mentally healthy. Such teachers, unable to draw on all of the functions in service of their students, become mired in a pattern of dysfunctional behavior that eventually deteriorates into a distortion of their preferred teaching style.

The new vision of the clinical cycle proposed in this book remains incomplete, because two important and closely related questions remain unanswered:

• How can ineffective teachers be helped to become more successful?

• How can professional growth be facilitated beyond perfecting the particular style that a teacher already exhibits?

One final time, in order to answer these questions, a popular movie will be consulted as a source of insight into the psychological dynamics of teaching. This particular film, entitled *Teachers,* illustrates the ineffective patterns of teaching described by Hanson and Silver (1998), but also suggests a path of transformation by which wholeness and integrity can be achieved.

Teachers, the Movie

The 1984 movie *Teachers* is an irreverent satire of public education, yet it also addresses serious matters on multiple levels. The main storyline revolves around a lawsuit brought by a former student who was allowed to graduate from the fictional John F. Kennedy High School without learning to read or write. At a deeper level, the film documents the maturation of a teacher as he comes to terms with neglected psychological functions, which are represented by other teachers in the film, and ultimately attains a fully integrated professional identity.

Early in the movie an attorney named Lisa Hammond, herself a graduate of JFK and now representing the student who has filed the lawsuit, arrives to explain that depositions for the case will be taken at the school. Recognizing her as a former student, the assistant principal brusquely responds that her problem has always been that she takes herself too seriously. Ironically and significantly, emblazoned on the office wall in huge letters behind him is the Delphic admonition to "Know Thy Self."

Getting to know and understand himself as a teacher is the fundamental problem facing Nick Nolte in the starring role of Alex Jurrell. We are introduced to Alex, a teacher with 15 years experience, as he is awakened in bed by a telephone call from the school secretary, who reminds him that it is Monday morning and he is already late. We see an empty beer can and a pack of cigarettes on his nightstand, and meet a young woman with whom he has evidently spent the night.

The young woman is surprised at what she overhears during the phone call, because Alex told her the night before that he was an airline pilot. When she asks if he is a teacher, he continues the deception by saying that the phone call was about a class he is scheduled to teach on "cabin pressure, you know, oxygen masks, things like that."

Coincidentally, Hanson and Silver (1998) use similar imagery to describe the situation of teachers and students whose dominant psychological function is exaggerated at the expense of the other three functions:

> It's similar to an aircraft that has lost some critical control device and is now plummeting through space in its own random way. A crash is virtually inevitable. The crash takes the form of what society calls neurosis or mental illness (p. 276).

The specific neuroses they identify include: depression, obsessive-compulsive disorder, hysteria, and dissociation.

Although a number of teachers are introduced in the movie, the viewer sees only four of them at work in their classrooms. None of the teachers is truly effective, however, because each is dominated by and relies upon a single exaggerated psychological function. In other words, they personify the neuroses that Hanson and Silver (1998) warn about.

The main character, Alex Jurrell, represents the dominant sensing function gone awry. His excessive smoking and drinking suggest serious depression and, figuratively, he appears to be ready to crash. Although Alex is popular with his students, he obviously and repeatedly neglects his duties. Instead of taking attendance, for example, he simply says to the class, "If you're not here, speak up." Looking after the students' physical comfort above their need to learn, he brings a tool box to school and begins repairing a broken radiator in the classroom, despite a student's loud complaint that "We're supposed to be learning about social studies, not radiators."

On another occasion, uncertain about how he will respond to questions posed at the upcoming deposition, Alex suggests that his class discuss the responsibility a school has to its community and to students. While these are certainly important questions that are appropriate for a social studies lesson, Alex isn't really teaching. Instead, he is trying to pry from students the meaning of teaching that he has forgotten over the years. Significantly, a student asks him, "Shouldn't we be going over our homework?" When the students' opinions about school are all negative, he gives them an assignment to "Tell me what is wrong with this school. Tell me what I should say." Consistent with his preference for sensing, Alex explains that the students can write a paper, take photographs, or sing a song, just as long as they communicate.

The next teacher we meet is nicknamed "Ditto," because the only thing that students do in his class is fill in purple worksheets. Significantly, early in the movie, he is attacked by the school psychologist, who is exasperated by his monopolizing of the ditto machine every morning. Enraged, she covers him with blue ditto fluid.

Ditto represents a perversion of the thinking function, manifested in obsessive-compulsive behavior. His classroom is arranged in straight rows, with his desk located at the back of the room. As soon as the bell rings at the start of class, the student seated in the last seat of each row silently stands up to get a stack of worksheets from the teacher's desk and passes them forward. Students spend the entire class period completing the worksheets without communicating with the teacher or other students. Ditto spends his time reading the newspaper and often dozing off. When the bell rings at the end of class, the students all rise and silently stack their completed worksheets on Ditto's desk as they file out of the room.

At one point in the film, Ditto boasts that for three consecutive years he has won teaching awards for having the most orderly class. One day, unknown to the students, Ditto dies quietly, asleep at his desk. At the end of class, the students routinely turn in their papers as they have been conditioned to do throughout the year. When the next class enters the room, monitors stand up, pick up stacks of worksheets to pass down each row, and the students get to work. It takes hours for someone to notice that Ditto is no longer alive.

The third teacher we meet is Carl Rosenberg, who displays characteristics of hysteria. Representing a dominant feeling function, the opposite of thinking, Carl criticizes Ditto's mechanical techniques and takes vicarious pleasure in his altercation with the school psychologist. But Carl is no more successful as a teacher than Ditto is. Students in his mathematics class sit in a U-shaped pattern, which increases communication among them but serves no instructional purpose. He is visibly nervous and frightened of the students and his class is entirely out of control. Carl alternately pleads with and shouts at the students to get their attention. They respond by playing pranks—changing the pronunciation of their names, hiding his desk, and stealing his car.

Underscoring his disdain for mechanical processes, in one scene Carl circulates around the classroom while students are working math problems and tells them that they are not allowed to use calculators. When Carl reaches in front of one student to point out an error, the student bites his hand hard enough to draw blood. Hearing screams, Nolte's character rushes to the rescue from the room next door and pries open the student's mouth. Carl wears a thick bandage on his hand for much of the remainder of the film. These events suggest that the teacher's feeling function has been wounded. In rendering assistance, Nolte's character takes a first step toward healing his own psyche by initiating an alliance between the sensing and feeling functions.

Perhaps the most memorable teacher in the movie, and the only one who comes close to being effective, is an outpatient from a mental hospital named Herbert, who is described as having "a few problems with reality." This character represents an exaggerated intuitive function manifested in a delusional state of dissociation.

After answering an incorrectly placed telephone call from the school secretary, Herbert eagerly accepts an invitation to serve as a substitute teacher. He begins his first lesson by asking the students, "Where did you leave off?" A student answers, saying, "Pickett's charge." Herbert begins to leaf through the textbook as if to locate the relevant section, then suddenly tosses the book out an open window. The students all respond with surprise, laughter, and applause.

Herbert then walks to a closet in a corner of the room and emerges dressed as Abraham Lincoln. He strides to the podium, silences students' jeers with a sober stare, pulls a rumpled envelope from his pocket, and begins reciting the Gettysburg address. The students listen quietly, enraptured by the solemn and inspiring words. Because of his delusional state, Herbert is able to access archetypal figures and events from American history. On other days, he teaches as Benjamin Franklin and re-enacts, with students, George Washington's crossing the Delaware with his troops.

On his first day at school, Herbert meets Carl and Alex in the corridor and asks them for directions to his classroom. This event signals further development of the teacher identity with the beginnings of a connection among the sensing, feeling, and intuiting functions. During one lesson, while dressed as General Custer, hospital orderlies arrive at the school and begin roughly escorting Herbert out of the classroom and down the hallway. In one of the most stirring moments in the film, Herbert suddenly stops, pulls his arms loose, and shouts, "Don't you know who I am?" One of the orderlies answers patronizingly, "Sure, you're General Custer." Herbert corrects him, saying sternly, "I am a *teacher!* And you will treat me as such."

Herbert proceeds down the hall unencumbered, his head held high. He pauses briefly and gently grasps Carl's wounded hand, then moves ahead and stops to greet Alex. Because they represent the opposing functions of intuiting and sensing, instead of shaking hands they stand at attention and salute while facing one another. Both smile broadly as they share a knowing look, suggesting that an important understanding has passed between them. Herbert walks out of the school, still dressed as General Custer, with the hospital orderlies trailing meekly behind him.

These events are significant in terms of an integration of psychological functions and illustrate Alex's ongoing development. Carl and Herbert represent parts of his fragmented psyche with which he is reconnecting. Intuition joins hands with wounded feeling. Sensing and intuition acknowledge each other as equals. No longer alive, the mechanical thinking function that Ditto represented is replaced by the attorney Lisa Hammond, with whom Alex gradually develops a romantic relationship. Lisa also represents an integration of a feminine element into Alex's personality.

At the end of the film, the lawsuit is settled for a large cash payment without going to court. The school board, administrators, and union representative, however, are intent on taking action to preserve public confidence. They plan to make Alex the scapegoat for a number of problems at the school and try to pressure him into resigning. His colleague Carl, who is the only person willing to speak truthfully about the district's lax promotion policy, is also being forced to resign.

Inspired by a spontaneous and very public display of support from Lisa, Alex not only refuses to accept the agreement that would end his teaching career, he also tears to shreds the document that Carl has reluctantly signed. At that very moment, Carl's missing car is returned, signifying that the feeling function is no longer immobilized and restricted. Incredulous over Alex's defiance, the superintendent says to him, "Jurrell! You're crazy. You know that?" To which Alex responds, "What can I say? I'm a teacher. I'm a teacher!" This final puzzling comment can be understood as the beginning of a new relationship between Alex's conscious ego and his unconscious mind. Jung (1976) described this "bringing together of opposites" as necessary for the emergence of what he termed the "transcendent function" (p. 295), experienced as "attaining liberation by one's own efforts and of finding the courage to be oneself" (p. 300). Having achieved a dynamic balance among all four psychological functions, Alex is now able to draw on his unconscious mind as a source of creativity and renewed energy. Jung warns that care must be taken at this point of the maturation process, because unconscious impulses can sometimes overwhelm and decenter the ego resulting in the risk of mental imbalance (1976, p. 296).

Application to Practice

The behaviors enacted in the movie *Teachers* are more than the idiosyncrasies of the four characters. Together, they are symptomatic of JFK High School's culture of alienation, apathy, disillusionment, and despair. Alex, the main character, personifies apathy, but he also represents an element of a dysfunctional school culture. He has lost touch with the passion and ideals that originally gave his job meaning and purpose, and now simply goes through the motions of teaching focused solely on the concrete experience.

Likewise, Carl's inattention to details and structure precipitate the practical jokes that his students play. His wounding symbolizes the inevitable disillusionment of a teacher guided solely by the feeling function. The substitute teacher, Herbert, engages students' attention, but his thinking and feeling functions are impaired. The alternative to the delusional fantasies he creates is profound despair. Finally, the teacher nicknamed Ditto is alienated from his students as human beings. Devoid of feeling and inspiration, his teaching is mechanical and sterile.

Fortunately, *Teachers* also suggests a way out of the ineffective culture manifested in these patterns of behavior. Lisa Hammond, the attorney, begins what might be considered a supervisory intervention when she engages both the school and Alex by confronting their apathy with the fact that students are not learning. She next establishes an empathic relationship with Alex, enabling him to connect with Carl and Herbert (as well as a troublesome student), who collectively symbolize the undeveloped feeling and intuiting functions. Lisa's encouragement of Alex and his own encouragement of Carl, results in their mutual empowerment and eventual victory over a dysfunctional school and system.

A "Cycle of Regeneration," based on this series of steps, is depicted in Figure 7.1. Could this cycle of engagement, empathy, encouragement, and empowerment serve to overcome a culture of alienation, apathy, discouragement, and despair in a real school? David Kolb's (1984) theory of experiential learning, published the same year that the movie *Teachers* was released, offers further clues as to how this might come about.

Figure 7.1

A Cycle of Regeneration

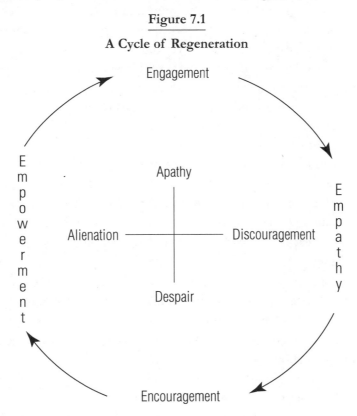

Experiential Learning Theory

On the basis of a design that is very similar to Jung's concept of psychological functions, Kolb (1984) identifies four types of learners that correspond closely to the *inventing, knowing, caring,* and *inspiring* teaching styles. Most people develop preferences for a particular style of learning, he believes, as a result of events in their lives, personality differences, environmental circumstances, and education. No style is necessarily better or worse than another, he insists. The important thing is to recognize that differences among learners do exist.

Kolb's learning theory has been used successfully with adults in a variety of settings, including higher education and training in organizations. His model portrays people as dynamic learners and problem solvers who constantly respond to their environments by engaging in new experiences, reflecting on these experiences from various perspectives, creating understandings and generalizations, and applying these understandings to their lives and to their work (Sims & Sims, 1995).

Integrating the wisdom of three great minds—John Dewey, Jean Piaget, and Kurt Lewin—Kolb (1984) proposes a recurring cycle of learning that includes four phases. The learning sequence begins with concrete experience, moves on to reflective observation, then to abstract conceptualization, and finally to active experimentation. The phases in this sequence build upon one another and reinforce the knowledge, skills, and dispositions learned at earlier phases. Thus, learning results from the wholistic engagement and interplay of affective, perceptual, cognitive, and behavioral processes. Modifying Kolb's learning cycle slightly to better account for the experiences of teaching gives us the dynamic illustrated in Figure 7.2. Teacher development can be understood as a recurring cycle of growth that begins with: a) concrete experience, followed by b) empathic reflection, c) construction of meaning, and d) active experimentation. As teachers progress through the learning cycle, they complement their initial teaching style with functions that have lain dormant. Integrating the styles allows them to recognize and enact a wider range of choices and decisions when facing new situations.

The phases of learning depicted in Figure 7.2 are best pursued with the support of a clinical coach or with a team of colleagues:

Phase 1: During the *concrete experience* phase of learning, the clinical coach actively engages the teacher in problem solving. Concrete data

Figure 7.2

Optimal Learning Environments for Promoting Teacher Development

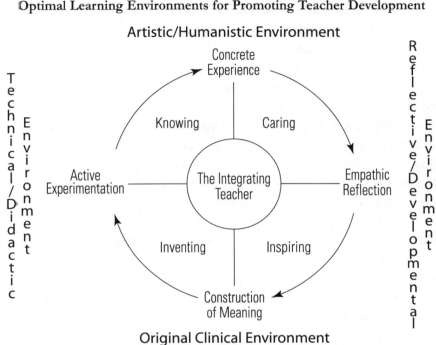

concerning teacher and student behavior, and their relationship to curriculum, standards, objectives, methods, materials, or classroom artifacts are considered. A key question during this phase is: "How well am I really doing?"

Phase 2: During the *empathic reflection* phase of learning, the coach displays and models empathy. Multiple perspectives are considered for the purpose of gaining insight into the subjective experience of students who inhabit the teacher's classroom. A question to ask during this phase is: "What is going on here for everyone involved?"

Phase 3: During the *construction of meaning* phase of learning, the clinical coach encourages the teacher to raise theoretical and ethical issues, form generalizations, and propose hypotheses concerning cause and effect relationships. The obvious central question for this phase is: "What does this all mean?"

Phase 4: During the *active experimentation* phase of learning, the coach steps back and empowers the teacher to take action. What has been learned is applied to practical problems in the classroom, accompanied by the collection of new data. The question guiding this phase is: "How can I do things better?"

Four distinct environments, also shown in Figure 7.2, have been proposed to facilitate learning during each of the four phases (Rainey & Kolb, 1995). These learning environments have the effect of gradually introducing people to psychological functions that are currently latent or little used. The environments also correspond to the four families of clinical supervision. An "affectively oriented" environment, which parallels the artistic/humanistic clinical family, is recommended during the *concrete experience* phase of learning. A "perceptionally oriented" environment, which aligns with the developmental/reflective clinical models, promotes learning during the *empathic reflection* phase. A "cognitively oriented" environment, corresponding to the original clinical models, is advised for the *construction of meaning* phase. Finally, a "behaviorally oriented" environment, paralleling the technical/didactic family of clinical models, is recommended to encourage learning during the *active experimentation* phase.

It should be noted that the learning environments encourage growth by gently nudging people out of their comfort zones. Teachers who exhibit a *knowing* style gradually learn to speak the language and dialects of an artistic/humanistic environment. Teachers who favor a *caring* style become acquainted with the language and dialects of a developmental/reflective environment. Teachers with an *inspiring* style, in turn, learn the language and dialects of the original clinical models. Finally, teachers who possess an *inventing* style become fluent in the language and dialects of a technical/didactic environment.

When embedded in the reality of classroom experience, alternative learning environments allow teachers to take greater responsibility for their own professional development. Teams of teachers might be organized in a school, as illustrated in Figure 7.3, according to their teaching style preferences. Individual teachers could rotate through different teams as they gain fluency with different languages and dialects, or entire teams could explore different learning environments together over a period of time. The purpose of such teams is not to "track" teachers, but to create within a school "a cooperative human community that cherishes and utilizes individual uniqueness" (Kolb, 1984, p. 62).

Figure 7.3

Alternative Environments for Professional Growth

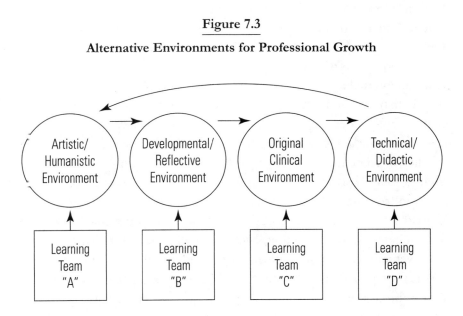

Closing Thoughts

The major implication of considering psychological functions and accommodating teaching style differences is that clinical supervisors must learn to interact with teachers in the manner that the teachers themselves learn best. Yet, much of what supervisors currently do, say, and think when they attempt to communicate with teachers is determined, consciously or unconsciously, by their own psychological preferences for perceiving and judging. Until supervisors become aware of their own style preferences and more sensitive to those of teachers, they will inadvertently favor, reward, and reinforce teachers who behave, speak, and think as they do, while misunderstanding and failing to communicate with teachers who differ from them.

Differentiating supervision according to teachers' psychological types is not a technique to be used from time to time, but is instead an entirely new way to supervise. Typically, we offer teachers a "take it or leave it" form of supervision, because we have a natural tendency to want teachers to teach their class the way we would do it if we were the teacher.

When I was a student in elementary school, during a less tolerant and enlightened age, some teachers forced their left-handed students to use their right hand when practicing cursive. The immediate result was that the left-handed children became frustrated and discouraged. Many, no doubt, became adults with illegible handwriting. Similarly, if a beginning teacher is forced to adopt a style of thinking and teaching by a supervisor who is unsympathetic, impatient, or inflexible, the teacher is likely to become frustrated and discouraged, and may never reach his or her full potential. Differentiating according to a style of teaching enables supervisors to help struggling teachers without relying on a remedial mentality.

Veteran teachers may initially have difficulty assuming responsibility for directing their own learning and challenging themselves to expand their repertoires. Time will certainly have to be spent ensuring that they find value in their own experiences and are able to apply new knowledge, skills, and dispositions as they broaden their professional practice. Although a particular style is likely to predominate and feel most natural, with enough practice in a supportive environment any teacher can master a variety of teaching styles.

Rather than advocating a particular way of behaving or thinking, the clinical supervisor in this new role facilitates learning by modeling alternative behaviors and patterns of thinking. At each phase of the learning cycle, he or she is: a) a colleague who models and supports conscious awareness of the personal experience of teaching, b) an empathic listener and sounding board who facilitates an understanding of the effect that teaching has on students, c) a knowledgeable resource who helps interpret subjective and objective information to arrive at moral and conceptual meaning, and d) a coach who empowers teachers toward action planning and hypothesis testing.

Attending to teacher differences requires flexibility in supervising and an environment that includes mutual respect, safety, shared responsibility for learning, and an emphasis on personal growth. Such change requires the supervisor to meet teachers where they are and then build on their strengths. In this way, the supervisor necessarily becomes more of a collegial coach. At a minimum, as a supervisor you need to

• Reflect on your own beliefs about learning, teaching, and supervision.

• Assess and reflect on the needs of the teacher as a learner.

• Be sensitive to preferences for perceiving and processing information, both the teacher's and your own.

• Clarify the new role of the clinical supervisor.

• Learn to use a variety of communication languages and dialects.

• Learn to use a range of supervisory approaches.

• Clarify the new role of the teacher.

• Begin building an inclusive community of learners.

It is true that schools are not structured for individualized supervision, but then neither are classrooms designed for individualized instruction. Differentiating supervision according to psychological type is worth the extra effort because it allows teachers to have a choice and a voice, which contributes to the coherence of their individual goals for professional development and is consistent with other reforms and classroom activities with which teachers are already involved.

Applying the languages and dialects of psychological type to instructional supervision forever alters the way that the clinical cycle is employed. The languages and dialects offer an alternative, more collegial and egalitarian, view of teaching and how it can be improved. Instead of a hierarchy of preferred behaviors or ways of thinking, we become aware that a broad range of teaching experiences exists, all of which are legitimate, acceptable, and valuable.

Discussion Questions

1. Are certain supervisory styles likely to work better with specific teaching styles? Do certain teaching and supervisory styles work better for attaining particular purposes?

2. Do effective supervisors adapt their style to match both the styles of teachers and the specific purposes they want to attain?

3. How can supervisors learn to adapt their supervisory styles to better address different teaching styles and purposes?

4. What advantages might be gained from teachers working together in learning environment teams? What disadvantages, if any, might result from this arrangement?

Appendix A: Clinical Dialect Preference Survey

Directions: Read the statement in italics and each item below. Circle the response from each pair that you would most prefer to have happen.

In a discussion with another person about teaching, I would prefer to:

1.   a. Spend a little time chatting before getting started.
          b. Focus on the topic as quickly as possible.

2.   a. Discuss how well my lesson plan worked.
          b. Come up with some new ideas that I can try.

3.   a. Keep the conversation factual and exact.
          b. Look at the "big picture."

4.   a. Consider "pros" and "cons" of different alternatives.
          b. Talk about how I feel about things as they come up.

5.   a. Maintain professional objectivity.
          b. Be warm and friendly.

6.   a. Talk about facts.
          b. Talk about ideas.

7.   a. Talk about values and beliefs.
          b. Use evidence and reasoning.

8. a. Interpret the meaning of what happened during a lesson.
    b. Talk about what was actually seen and heard during a lesson.

9. a. Get objective information about teaching.
    b. Get affirmation for what I am doing in my classroom.

10. a. Describe observable behaviors first, then identify the patterns.
    b. Discuss a general idea first, then work out the details.

11. a. Get a quick overview of key ideas.
    b. Thoroughly understand the details.

12. a. Talk about values.
    b. Talk about standards of achievement.

13. a. Consider a lesson in its entirety.
    b. Consider each part of the lesson separately.

14. a. Make decisions based on what I feel is right.
    b. Make decisions based on logical analysis.

15. a. Raise challenging questions.
    b. Maintain a positive relationship.

16. a. Get some practical ideas that I can use in my classroom.
    b. Get ideas that broaden my understanding of teaching.

17. a. Talk about what could possibly happen.
    b. Talk about what actually did happen.

18. a. Keep the discussion friendly and personal.
    b. Keep the discussion objective and professional.

19.   a. Identify goals and purposes.
        b. Express my feelings.

20.   a. "Fine tune" my teaching.
        b. Develop an understanding of teaching.

21.   a. Be logical.
        b. Find out what we agree about.

22.   a. Talk about principles.
        b. Talk about facts.

23.   a. Consider the influence of alternatives on students or other people.
        b. Keep the conference brief and concise.

24.   a. Talk about specific examples.
        b. Talk about future lessons.

25.   a. Rely mostly on logic and analysis.
        b. Spend time talking about things that are personally important.

26.   a. Talk about what is concrete and real.
        b. Consider original ideas and theories.

Clinical Dialect Preference Scoring Guide

First: Circle the response that you gave for each item on the survey. Note that the items below are not listed in numerical order.

1.	A ———- B	2.	A ———- B	
4.	B ———-A	3.	A ———- B	
5.	B ———-A	6.	A ———- B	
7.	A ———- B	8.	B ———-A	
9.	B ———-A	10.	A ———- B	
12.	A ———- B	11.	B ———-A	
14.	A ———- B	13.	B ———-A	
15.	B ———-A	16.	A ———- B	
18.	A ———- B	17.	B ———-A	
19.	B ———-A	20.	A ———- B	
21.	B ———-A	22.	B ———-A	
23.	A ———- B	24.	A ———- B	
25.	B ———-A	26.	A ———- B	

_____   _____ Totals   _____   _____ Totals
  F   **T**   **S**   **N**

Second: Add the number of circled responses in each column of letters and write the totals on the lines at the bottom of each column.

Third: Find the highest column total, then draw an asterisk (*) next to the letter that is printed just below that number (F, T, S, or N).

Fourth: Find the second highest column total, then draw two asterisks (**) next to the letter that is just below that number (F, T, S, or N).

Interpretation: The letter with a single asterisk represents the psychological function (feeling, thinking, sensing, or intuiting) that you rely on initially and most often when communicating orally. The letter with two asterisks is the function that you rely on second. The two functions without asterisks are used infrequently, if at all, because they are comparatively undeveloped.

Appendix B: Communicating with Teachers Worksheets

Communicating with *Inventing* Teachers
(Discovering or Problem-Solving Style)

As a _____ clinical supervisor, how should I work with an
     (your clinical dialect)

inventing teacher?

How does my communication style make me a good supervisor for *inventing* teachers?

How will my communication style frustrate *inventing* teachers?

Where do I need to be more flexible when working with an *inventing* teacher?

When we work together, where are we likely to encounter blindspots?

What do I want to say to this teacher? How will I say it?

What do I want to ask this teacher? How will I ask it?

How do I phrase my communication in a "language" that an *inventing* teacher will most readily understand?

Communicating with *Knowing* Teachers
(Law-Giving or Organizing Style)

As a _____ clinical supervisor, how should I work
      (your clinical dialect)
with a *knowing* teacher?

How does my communication style make me a good supervisor for *knowing* teachers?

How will my communication style frustrate *knowing* teachers?

Where do I need to be more flexible when working with a *knowing* teacher?

When we work together, where are we likely to encounter blindspots?

What do I want to say to this teacher? How will I say it?

What do I want to ask this teacher? How will I ask it?

How do I phrase my communication in a "language" that a *knowing* teacher will most readily understand?

Communicating with *Caring* Teachers (Orchestrating or Caregiving Style)

As a _____ clinical supervisor, how should I work with a
(your clinical dialect)

caring teacher?

How does my communication style make me a good supervisor for *caring* teachers?

How will my communication style frustrate *caring* teachers?

Where do I need to be more flexible when working with a *caring* teacher?

When we work together, where are we likely to encounter blindspots?

What do I want to say to this teacher? How will I say it?

What do I want to ask this teacher? How will I ask it?

How do I phrase my communication in a "language" that a *caring* teacher will most readily understand?

Communicating with *Inspiring* Teachers
(Idealizing or Liberating Style)

As a _____ clinical supervisor, how should I work with an
(your clinical dialect)

inspiring teacher?

How does my communication style make me a good supervisor for *inspiring* teachers?

How will my communication style frustrate *inspiring* teachers?

Where do I need to be more flexible when working with an *inspiring* teacher?

When we work together, where are we likely to encounter blindspots?

What do I want to say to this teacher? How will I say it?

What do I want to ask this teacher? How will I ask it?

How do I phrase my communication in a "language" that an *inspiring* teacher will most readily understand?

Note: These worksheets are adapted from *Developing your "coachee" through his/her type,* by K. G. Ridout, 2001, Raleigh, NC: Wellspring Consulting.

References

Acheson, K. A., & Gall, M. D. (1980). *Techniques in the clinical supervision of teachers.* White Plains, NY: Longman.

Ayer, F. C., & Barr, A. S. (1928). *The organization of supervision: An analysis of the organization and administration of supervision in city school systems.* New York: Appleton.

Barr, A. S., & Burton, W. H. (1926). *The supervision of instruction.* New York: Appleton-Century.

Blumberg, A. (1974). *Supervisors and teachers: A private cold war.* Berkeley, CA: McCutchan.

Briggs, K. A., & Myers, I. B. (1977). *Myers-Briggs Type Indicator.* Palo Alto, CA: Consulting Psychologists Press.

Burton, W. H. (1927). *Supervision and the improvement of teaching.* New York: Appleton-Century.

Callahan, R. E. (1962). *Education and the cult of efficiency.* Chicago: University of Chicago Press.

Callahan, R. E., & Button, H. W. (1964). Historical change of the role of the man in the organization: 1865–1950. In D. E. Griffiths, (Ed.), *Behavioral science and educational administration,* The Sixty-third Yearbook of the National Society for the Study of Education, Part II. Chicago: University of Chicago Press.

Campbell, J. (1949). *The hero with a thousand faces.* Princeton, NJ: Princeton University Press.

Champagne, D. W., & Hogan, R. C. (1995). *Consultant supervision: Theory and skill development* (3rd ed.). Wheaton, IL: CH Publications.

Cogan, M. L. (1973). *Clinical supervision.* Boston: Houghton Mifflin.

Collins, M., & Tamarkin, C. (1990). *Marva Collins' Way.* New York: Jeremy P. Tarcher/Perigree Books.

Costa, A. L., & Garmston, R. J. (1994). *Cognitive coaching: A foundation for renaissance schools.* Norwood, MA: Christopher-Gordon.

Danielson, C. (1996). *Enhancing professional practice: A framework for teaching.* Alexandria, VA: ASCD.

Eisner, E. W. (1979). *The educational imagination: On the design and evaluation of educational programs.* New York: Macmillan.

Eisner, E. W., & Vallance, E. (1974). *Conflicting conceptions of curriculum.* Berkeley, CA: McCutchan.

Elliott, E. C. (1914). *City school supervision.* New York: World Book.

Fitzgerald, C., & Kirby, L. (Eds.). (1997). *Developing leaders: Research and applications in psychological type and leadership development.* Palo Alto, CA: Davies-Black.

Garman, N. B. (1986). Reflection, the heart of clinical supervision: A modern rationale for practice. *Journal of Curriculum and Supervision, 2*(1), 1-24.

Garmston, R. J., Lipton, L. E., & Kaiser, K. (1998). The psychology of supervision. In G. R. Firth and E. F. Pajak (Eds.), *Handbook of research on school supervision* (pp. 242-286). New York: Simon & Schuster Macmillan.

Glickman, C. D. (1985). *Supervision of instruction: A developmental approach.* Boston: Allyn & Bacon.

Glickman, C. D. (2001, October). Dichotomizing school reform: Why no one wins and America loses. *Phi Delta Kappan, 83,* 147-152.

Goldhammer, R. (1969). *Clinical supervision: Special methods for the supervision of teachers.* New York: Holt, Rinehart & Winston.

Gregorc, A. (1982). *An adult's guide to style.* Maynard, MA: Gabriel Systems.

Grimmett, P. P. (1989). A commentary on Schon's view of reflection. *Journal of Curriculum and Supervision, 5* (1), 19-28.

Hanson, J. R., & Silver, H. F. (1998). *Learning styles and strategies* (3rd ed.). Woodbridge, NJ: Silver, Strong, & Associates.

Harris, B. M., & Hill, J. (1982). *Developmental teacher evaluation kit.* Austin, TX: Southwest Educational Development Laboratory.

Hawthorne, R. D., & Hoffman, N. E. (1998). Supervision in non-teaching professions. In Gerald R. Firth and Edward F. Pajak (Eds.), *Handbook of research on school supervision,* pp. 555-580. New York: Simon & Schuster Macmillan.

Hilton, J. (1986). *Goodbye, Mr. Chips.* New York: Bantam Books.

Hirsch, S. K., & Kummerow, J. M. (1998). *Introduction to type in organizations.* Palo Alto, CA: Consulting Psychologists Press.

Hopcke, R. H. (1999). *A guided tour of the collected works of C. G. Jung.* Boston: Shambhala.

Hosic, J. F. (1920). The democratization of supervision. *School and Society, 11,* 331-336.

Hunter, M. (1984). Knowing, teaching, and supervising. In P. L. Holford (Ed.), *Using what we know about teaching.* Alexandria, VA: ASCD.

Joyce, B., & Weil, M. (1972). *Models of teaching.* Englewood Cliffs, NJ: Prentice Hall.

Joyce, B., & Weil, M. (1986). *Models of teaching* (3rd ed.). Englewood Cliffs, NJ: Prentice Hall.

Jung, C. G. (1969). *Archetypes and the collective unconscious.* Princeton, NJ: Princeton University Press.

Jung, C. G. (1971). *Psychological types.* A revision by R. F. C. Hull of the translation by H. G. Baynes. Princeton, NJ: Princeton University Press.

Jung, C. G. (1976).The transcendent function. In J. Campbell (Ed.), *The portable Jung.* New York: Penguin Books.

Jung, C. G. (1979). *Man and his symbols.* New York: Dell.

Keirsey, D. (1998). *Please understand me II: Temperament, character, intelligence.* Del Mar, CA: Prometheus Nemisis.

Kolb, D. A. (1984). *Experiential learning.* Englewood Cliff, NJ: Prentice Hall.

Kroeger, O., & Thuesen, J. M. (1988). *Type talk: Or how to determine your personality type and change your life.* New York: Delacorte Press.

Marva Collins Seminars, Inc. (2002). *Marva Collins Biography.* http://www.marvacollins.com/biography.html

McCarthy, B. (1982). Improving staff development through CBAM and 4MAT. *Educational Leadership, 40* (1), 20-25.

McCarthy, B. (1990). Using the 4MAT system to bring learning styles to schools. *Educational Leadership, 48* (2), 31-37.

Mosston, M., & Ashworth, S. (1990). *The spectrum of teaching styles: From command to discovery.* New York: Longman.

Myers-Briggs Type Indicator Step II. (1996). Palo Alto, CA: Consulting Psychologists Press.

Norris, C. J. (1991). Supervising with style. *Theory Into Practice, 30* (Spring 1991), 129-133.

Oja, S. N., & Reiman, A. J. (1998). Supervision for teacher development across the career span. In G. R. Firth and E. F. Pajak (Eds.), *Handbook of research on school supervision*, pp. 463-487. New York: Simon & Schuster Macmillan.

Ornstein, A. C., & Hunkins, F. P. (1998). *Curriculum: Foundations, principles, and theory*, (3rd ed.). Boston: Allyn & Bacon.

Pajak, E. F. (2000). *Approaches to clinical supervision: Alternatives for improving instruction* (2nd ed.). Norwood, MA: Christopher-Gordon.

Pajak, E. F. (2002). From the Classics: *Goodbye, Mr. Chips. The San Francisco Jung Institute Library Journal, 21* (1) 1-11.

Patton, F. G. (1954). *Good morning, Miss Dove.* New York: Dodd, Meade & Company.

PersonalityType.com (2001). *The Art of Speedreading People.* http://personalitytype.com/index.html

Rainey, M. A., & Kolb, D. A. (1995). Using experiential learning theory and learning styles in diversity education. In, R. R. Sims & S. J. Sims (Eds.), *The importance of learning styles.* Westport, CT: Greenwood Press.

Reinsmith, W. A. (1992). *Archetypal Forms in Teaching: A Continuum.* New York: Greenwood Press.

Ridout, K. G. (2001). *Developing your "coachee" through his/her type.* Raleigh, NC: Wellspring Consulting.

Sergiovanni, T. J. (1995). The politics of virtue: A new framework for school leadership. *The School Community Journal, 5* Fall/Winter 1995, 13–22.

Sergiovanni, T. J., & Starratt, R. J. (1998). *Supervision: A redefinition,* (6th ed.). Boston, McGraw Hill.

Shapiro, A. S., & Blumberg, A. (1998). Social dimensions of supervision. In G. R. Firth and E. F. Pajak (Eds.), *Handbook of research on school supervision,* pp. 1055–1084. New York: Simon & Schuster Macmillan.

Silver, H., Strong, R., & Perini, M. (2000). *So each may learn: Integrating learning styles and multiple intelligences.* Alexandria, VA: ASCD.

Sims, R. R., & Sims, S. J. (1995). *The importance of learning styles.* Westport, CT: Greenwood Press.

Smith, D., & Kolb, D. A. (1985). *User guide for the learning-style inventory: A manual for teachers and trainers.* Boston, MA: McBer and Company.

Smyth, J. W. (1985). Developing a critical practice of clinical supervision. *Journal of Curriculum and Supervision, 17* (January–March), 1–15.

Stevens, A. (1994). *Jung: A very short introduction.* Oxford, England: Oxford University Press.

Stone, C. R. (1929). *Supervision of the elementary school.* Boston: Houghton-Mifflin.

Thompson, H. L. (2000). *Introduction to the communicationwheel.* Watkinsville, GA: Wormhole Publishing.

Waite, D. (1995). *Rethinking instructional supervision: Notes on its language and culture.* Washington, DC: Falmer Press.

Zeichner, K. M., & Liston, D. P. (1987). Teaching students to reflect. *Harvard Educational Review, 57* (February), 23–48.

Zeichner, K. M., & Liston, D. P. (1996). *Reflective teaching: An introduction.* Mahwah, NJ: Erlbaum.

Movie
References

The Beautician and the Beast (1997). Paramount Pictures.

Dangerous Minds (1995). Hollywood Pictures.

Dead Poets Society (1989). Touchstone Pictures.

Goodbye, Mr. Chips (1939). Metro Goldwyn Mayer.

Good Morning, Miss Dove (1955). 20th Century Fox.
     (not available on VHS or DVD)

Kindergarten Cop (1990). Image Entertainment.

The Marva Collins Story (1981). CBS Special Movie.
     (not available on VHS or DVD)

Mr. Holland's Opus (1995). Miramax Films.

Music of the Heart (1999). Miramax Films.

Pay It Forward (2000). Warner Brothers Pictures.

The Paper Chase (1973). 20th Century Fox.

Stand and Deliver (1988). Warner Brothers Pictures.

Teachers (1984). MGM/United Artists.

To Sir, with Love (1967). Columbia Pictures.

Index

In this index, page locators followed by *f* indicate a figure found in the text.

Acheson, K. A., 39–40
administration, scientific management
  movement in, 5
archetypes and teachers, 34–35, 84
artistic-humanistic (S-F) teachers
  clinical supervision model, 8–9, 19*f*
  dialect of, 38*f*, 40–42, 73
  environment for development of, 89*f*,
    90, 91*f*
  new vision cycle of supervision for, 64*f*

The Beautician and the Beast, 32
best practice conversation example, 1–3,
  50–51
Blumberg, Arthur, 40–42, 45

Callahan, Raymond, 4–5
Campbell, Joseph, 27
care-giving dialect. *See* F-S (humanistic-
  artistic) teachers, dialect of
caring teachers
  described, 23, 24, 31
  environment best for learning, 89*f*, 90
  function pairs of, 28*f*
  language/communication dialects of,
    38*f*, 40–42
  movies depicting, 28*f*, 31–32
  new vision cycle of supervision for,
    64*f*, 71–73
Champagne, D.W., 10
classroom observation, in the five-stage
  model, 6
Clinical Language Circle
  applications, 59–61
  concept, 48–51, 49*f*
  portfolio review example, 52–59, 57*f*

clinical supervision. *See also* teacher
  development
  assessment recommendations, 63
  background, 5
  Cycle of Regeneration, 87*f*
  democracy principle in, 4–5, 37
  example in *Teachers*, 86
  five-stage sequence, 6–7, 64*f*
  new vision characteristics, 62–63,
    92–94
  new vision cycle, 64*f*, 68–76
clinical supervision, four families of. *See
  also specific models* e.g. reflective-
  developmental (N-F)
  Clinical Language Circle and, 48–51
  function pairs related to, 19–21, 19*f*
  learning environments linked, 90, 91*f*
  overview, 7–9
clinical supervision, new vision cycle. *See
  also* teacher development
  caring teachers, 64*f*, 71–73
  inspiring teachers, 64*f*, 74–76
  inventing teachers, 64*f*
  knowing teachers, 64*f*, 68–70
Cogan, Morris, 5, 8, 37–39
communication. *See also*
  language/communication dialects
  best practice conversation example,
    1–3, 50–51
  Clinical Language Circle, 48–51, 49*f*
  portfolio review example, 52–59, 57*f*
  psychological functions influence on,
    36, 43–44, 49–51
communication dialect information flow,
  44–47, 50
conference, in the five-stage model, 7

Costa, A. L., 42–43
curriculum, four philosophies (Ornstein
   and Hunkins), 25
Cycle of Regeneration, 87*f*

Dangerous Minds, 33–34
data analysis, in the five-stage model, 6–7
Dead Poets Society, 33
depression and the sensing function, 81–82
developmental-reflective (N-F) teachers
   clinical supervision model, 8–9, 19*f*
   dialect of, 38*f*, 42–43, 76–77
   new vision cycle of supervision for, 64*f*
   portfolio review example, 52–59, 57*f*
dialects of language/communication. *See*
   language/communication dialects
didactic-technical (T-S) teachers
   dialect of, 38*f*, 39–40, 70
   new vision cycle of supervision for, 64*f*
   portfolio review example, 52–59, 57*f*
discovering dialect. *See* N-T (intuiting-
   thinking) teachers, dialect of

Education and the Cult of Efficiency
   (Callahan), 5
Eisner, Elliott, 40–42
Elliott, Edward C., 4
experiential learning theory, 87–91

feeling (F) function, 11, 16, 83
five-stage sequence of clinical supervision,
   6–7, 64*f*
F-N (reflective-developmental) teachers
   dialect of, 38*f*, 42–43, 77
   environment for development of, 89*f*,
     90, 91*f*
   new vision cycle of supervision for, 64*f*
   portfolio review example, 52–59, 57*f*
four families of clinical supervision. *See*
   clinical supervision, four families of
four groups of teaching models (Joyce and
   Weil), 25
four orientations of instruction (Joyce and
   Weil), 25

four philosophies of curriculum (Ornstein
   and Hunkins), 25
four psychological functions (Jung). *See*
   psychological functions (four) of Jung
four psychological perspectives of lessons
   in the classroom, 15–17
four teaching styles (Pajak). *See* teaching
   styles, four models (Pajak)
F-S (humanistic-artistic) teachers
   dialect of, 38*f*, 40–42, 74
   new vision cycle of supervision for, 64*f*
function pairs. *See also individual
   function pairs*; psychological functions
   (four) of Jung
   clinical supervision families related to,
     19–21, 19*f*
   combinations of, 19–20, 19*f*
   as dialects, 36–37
   four teaching styles of Pajak
     connected, 23–24

Gall, M. D., 39–40
Garmston, R. J., 42–43
Glickman, C. D., 42–43
Goldhammer, Robert, 5–6, 8, 37, 39, 45
Goodbye, Mr. Chips, 32
Good Morning, Miss Dove, 30–31

Hanson, J. R., 79–81
hero
   archetypes of teacher as, 34–35, 84
   story of the, 27, 79
The Hero with a Thousand Faces
   (Campbell), 27
Hogan, R. C., 10
humanistic-artistic (F-S) teachers
   dialect of, 38*f*, 40–42, 74
   new vision cycle of supervision for, 64*f*
Hunter, M., 40, 45
hysteria and the feeling function, 83

idealizing dialect. *See* F-N (reflective-
   developmental) teachers, dialect of
information processing, thinking/feeling
   function in, 14

inspiring teachers
    described, 24, 33
    environment best for learning, 89*f*, 90
    function pairs of, 28*f*
    language/communication dialects of,
      38*f*, 42–43
    movies depicting, 29*f*, 33–34
    new vision cycle of supervision for,
      64*f*, 74–76
instructional supervision. *See* clinical
    supervision
intuiting (N) function, 11, 17, 83–85
intuiting-thinking (N-T) function pair, 20
intuiting-thinking (N-T) teachers
    (original) model of clinical supervision,
      8–9, 19*f*
    dialect of, 37–39, 38*f*, 67
    environment for development of, 89*f*,
      90, 91*f*
    new vision cycle of supervision for, 64*f*
    portfolio review example, 52–59, 57*f*
intuitive-feeling (N-F) function pair, 20
inventing teachers
    clinical supervision cycle, 63–67
    described, 23, 24, 28–29
    environment best for learning, 89*f*, 90
    function pairs of, 28*f*
    language/communication dialects of,
      37–39, 38*f*
    movies depicting, 28*f*, 29
    new vision cycle of supervision for, 64*f*

Jung, Carl, 10–11. *See also* psychological
    functions (four) of Jung

Keirsey, D., 39, 42
Kindergarten Cop, 30
knowing teachers
    described, 23, 24, 30
    environment best for learning, 89*f*, 90
    function pairs of, 28*f*
    language/communication dialects of,
      38*f*, 39–40
    movies depicting, 28*f*, 30–31

knowing teachers (*continued*)
    new vision cycle of supervision for,
      64*f*, 68–70
Kolb, David, 87–88

language/communication dialects. *See also*
    specific dialects
    of four psychological functions (Jung),
      36–37, 38*f*
    information flow, 44–47
law-giving dialect. *See* T-S (technical-
    didactic) teachers, dialect of
learning theory, experiential, 87–91
lessons in the classroom, four
    psychological perspectives of, 15–17
liberating dialect. *See* N-F (developmental-
    reflective) teachers, dialect of
Liston, D. P., 42

Man and His Symbols (Jung), 11
The Marva Collins Story, 31
movies. *See also* specific titles
    list of titles used as examples, 112
    professional growth modeled by, 80–87
    teaching styles represented by, 28*f*
Mr. Holland's Opus, 32
Music of the Heart, 31–32
My Posse Don't Do Homework (Johnson),
    33

N-F (developmental-reflective) teachers
    clinical supervision model, 8–9, 19*f*
    dialect of, 38*f*, 42–43, 76–77
    new vision cycle of supervision for, 64*f*
    portfolio review example, 52–59, 57*f*
N-F (intuitive-feeling) function pair, 20
N (intuiting) function, 11, 17, 83–85
N-T (intuiting-thinking) teachers
    (original) model of clinical supervision,
      8–9, 19*f*
    dialect of, 37–39, 38*f*, 67
    environment for development of, 89*f*,
      90, 91*f*
    new vision cycle of supervision for, 64*f*
    portfolio review example, 52–59, 57*f*

N-T (intuiting-thinking) teachers (*continued*)
N-T (intuitive-thinking) function pair, 20

obsessive-compulsive behavior and the thinking function, 82–83
orchestrating dialect. *See* S-F (artistic-humanistic) teachers, dialect of
organizing dialect. *See* S-T (didactic-technical) teachers, dialect of
original clinical model (N-T) of supervision concept, 8–9
    environment for development of, 89*f*, 90, 91*f*
    function pairs of, 19*f*
    language/communication dialects of, 37–39, 38*f*

The Paper Chase, 30
Pay It Forward, 32
portfolio review example, 52–59, 57*f*
postconference analysis, in the five-stage model,
pre-observation conference, in the five-stage model, 6
problem-solving dialect. *See* T-N (thinking-intuiting) teachers, dialect of
professional development. *See* clinical supervision; teacher development
psychological functions (four) of Jung. *See also specific functions* and *specific function pairs*
    classroom observation perspectives, 15–17
    concept, 10–11, 12*f*
    dominant/supporting functions, 17
    four teaching styles connected, 24*f*
    integration example, 85–86
    interaction analogy, 17–18
    language/communication dialects of, 36–37, 38*f*
    shadow function, 17
    understanding communication with, 36, 43–47, 49–51
psychological temperament classification

psychological functions (four) of Jung (*continued*)
    scheme, 39

reflective-developmental (F-N) teachers
    dialect of, 38*f*, 42–43, 77
    environment for development of, 89*f*, 90, 91*f*
    new vision cycle of supervision for, 64*f*
    portfolio review example, 52–59, 57*f*
Regeneration, Cycle of, 87*f*

sensing-intuiting (S-N) function pair, 11–13
sensing (S) function, 11, 15, 81–82
sensory-feeling (S-F) function pair, 20
sensory-thinking (S-T) function pair, 20
S-F (artistic-humanistic) teachers
    clinical supervision model, 8–9, 19*f*
    dialect of, 38*f*, 40–42, 73
    environment for development of, 89*f*, 90, 91*f*
    new vision cycle of supervision for, 64*f*
S-F (sensory-feeling) function pair, 20
Silver, H. F., 79–81
To Sir with Love, 29
sixth sense. *See* intuiting (N) function
Smyth, J. W., 42
S-N (sensing-intuiting) function pair, 11–13
S (sensing) function, 11, 15, 81–82
Stand and Deliver, 29
strategy, in the five-stage model, 6–7
S-T (sensory-thinking) function pair, 20
S-T (technical-didactic) function pair, 20
S-T (technical-didactic) teachers
    clinical supervision model, 8–9, 19*f*
    dialect of, 38*f*, 39–40, 70–71
    environment for development of, 89*f*, 90, 91*f*
    new vision cycle of supervision for, 64*f*
S-T (technical) outcome/growth dimension, 59
supervision, clinical. *See* clinical supervision

teacher development. *See also* clinical
supervision
  example in *Teachers*, 80-87
  learning environments promoting, 89*f*,
    90-91, 91*f*
  learning growth cycle phases, 88-90
Teachers, 80-87
teachers and archetypes, 34-35, 84
teaching models, four orientations (Joyce
  and Weil), 25
teaching styles, four models (Pajak). *See
also specific teaching styles*
  development of, 22-23
  four curriculum philosophies
    connected, 24-25
  four orientations of instruction
    connected, 25
  four psychological styles connected,
    23-24, 24*f*
  movies depicting, 28*f*
  patterns identified in, 26*f*
  subcategories of experience, 28*f*
technical-didactic (S-T) function pair, 20
technical-didactic (S-T) teachers
  clinical supervision model, 8-9, 19*f*

technical-didactic (S-T) teachers
  (*continued*)
  dialect of, 38*f*, 39-40, 70-71
  environment for development of, 89*f*,
    90, 91*f*
  new vision cycle of supervision for, 64*f*
*Techniques in the Clinical Supervision of
  Teachers* (Acheson and Gall), 38*f*
thinking-intuiting (T-N) teachers
  dialect of, 37-39, 38*f*, 67
  new vision cycle of supervision for, 64*f*
thinking (T) function, 11, 13-14, 16, 82-83
Thompson, H. L., 34-36, 48-50
T-N (thinking-intuiting) teachers
  dialect of, 37-39, 38*f*, 67
  new vision cycle of supervision for, 64*f*
T-S (didactic-technical) teachers
  dialect of, 38*f*, 39-40, 70
  new vision cycle of supervision for, 64*f*
  portfolio review example, 52-59, 57*f*
T (thinking) function, 11, 13-14, 16, 82-83

Waite, D., 42

Zeichner, K. M., 42

About the Author

Edward Pajak is a professor and chair of the Department of Teacher Development and Leadership at Johns Hopkins University. He earned his bachelor's degree at the State University of New York at Buffalo and began his teaching career at the middle school level in the Buffalo and Syracuse areas. After completing a master's and doctoral degree at Syracuse University, he served on the faculties of Virginia Commonwealth University and the University of Georgia, as well as in several administrative positions.

Before moving to Johns Hopkins in 2001, Dr. Pajak led a systemic educational improvement effort in Northeast Georgia involving collaboration among institutions of higher education, local community groups, and PreK–12 schools. He also served for two years as co-director of Georgia's statewide Teacher Quality Plan. Dr. Pajak has published more than 40 articles in professional journals, most recently, the *Journal of Curriculum and Supervision*, the *Journal of Teacher Education*, and the *San Francisco Jung Institute Library Journal*. He has authored and co-edited four books, including: *Approaches to Clinical Supervision: Alternatives for Improving Instruction* (Christopher-Gordon); *Contemporary Issues in Curriculum* (Allyn and Bacon); the *Handbook of Research on School Supervision* (Macmillan); and *The Central Office Supervisor of Curriculum and Instruction: Setting the Stage for Success* (Allyn and Bacon). Dr. Pajak currently serves as president of the Council of Professors of Instructional Supervision.

Dr. Pajak may be contacted at:

105 Whitehead Hall
Johns Hopkins University
3400 North Charles St.
Baltimore, MD 21218
410-516-8274
epajak@jhu.edu